They Call It Love

They Call It Love

The Politics of Emotional Life

Alva Gotby

VERSO

London • New York

First published by Verso 2023
© Alva Gotby 2023

1 3 5 7 9 10 8 6 4 2

Verso
UK: 6 Meard Street, London W1F 0EG
US: 388 Atlantic Avenue, Brooklyn, NY 11217
versobooks.com

Verso is the imprint of New Left Books

ISBN-13: 978-1-83976-703-6
ISBN-13: 978-1-83976-705-0 (UK EBK)
ISBN-13: 978-1-83976-706-7 (US EBK)

British Library Cataloguing in Publication Data
A catalogue record for this book is available from the British Library

Library of Congress Cataloging-in-Publication Data
Names: Gotby, Alva, author.
Title: They call it love : the politics of emotional life / Alva Gotby.
Description: London ; New York : Verso, [2022] | Includes bibliographical
    references.
Identifiers: LCCN 2022033522 (print) | LCCN 2022033523 (ebook) | ISBN
    9781839767036 (hardback) | ISBN 9781839767067 (US ebook) | ISBN
    9781839767050 (UK ebook)
Subjects: LCSH: Work—Psychological aspects. | Capitalism—Psychological
    aspects. | Women caregivers—Psychology. | Women caregivers—Social
    conditions. | Feminist theory.
Classification: LCC BF531 .G68 2022 (print) | LCC BF531 (ebook) | DDC
    152.4/1—dc23/eng/20220921
LC record available at https://lccn.loc.gov/2022033522
LC ebook record available at https://lccn.loc.gov/2022033523

Typeset in Sabon by Hewer Text UK Ltd, Edinburgh
Printed and bound by CPI Group (UK) Ltd, Croydon CR0 4YY

To my friends

Moments of taking charge of ourselves foreground themselves in a lot of forgettable necessity. An interesting story is made of agency, but humans exist as fully on this shadow side of helplessness as we do on the daylight side of doing what we want. To be cared for is the invisible substructure of autonomy, the necessary work brought about by the weakness of a human body across the span of life. Our gaze into the world is sometimes a needy one, a face that says 'love me,' by which it means something like 'bring me some soup.'

—Anne Boyer, *The Undying*

Contents

Introduction

How do you know you are loved? How do you know someone cares for you? Think about the small gestures of love – all
the little things that have made you feel cared for. Think about
the times that felt nice, when you experienced the emotional
warmth of being with other people. Who was creating that
feeling? Who was working to make you feel safe, loved, and
supported?

The work of caring for people is an essential but disavowed
and devalued aspect of capitalist societies. Without the labour
of ensuring that most people feel well enough to keep going to
work, capitalism could not function. Capitalist society
produces a lot of suffering, but many people work hard to
alleviate one another's pain, stress, and boredom. At the same
time, this work creates emotional attachments not only to
other people but to the world as we know it.

This book is about the politics of reproductive labour – that
is, the work that goes into maintaining and replacing the labour
force and ensuring people's wellbeing. This work includes both
generational replacement, such as pregnancy and childcare, and
the daily work of cooking, cleaning, doing laundry, and caring
for the sick, disabled, and elderly. These forms of work are
often referred to as social reproduction. A less visible form of
reproduction is emotional support – comforting those who feel
angry or sad, cheering up a family member or friend, or creating a general spirit of niceness at home or at work. It also
involves the work of building and maintaining communities
and social relations. Emotion is essential for the reproduction
of the workforce and for producing forms of sociality and

subjectivity. Reproductive labour has an important emotional aspect – the work of soothing children, providing company for the elderly, and maintaining intimate forms of sociality. This work is commonly known as 'love'.

Emotion forms an integral part of social reproduction more broadly – it is a key part of reproductive work. Therefore, I propose that we call this work 'emotional reproduction'. Emotional reproduction is not something we usually think about or notice. It is the everyday work that we do for our family members, friends, co-workers, and others – cheering up those who are feeling sad or lonely, creating emotional warmth. There is an assumption in our society that healthy adults can care for themselves and that only children and people with a mental illness need emotional support. But we are all dependent on one another. Adults as well as children need emotional care. And not only those with a mental illness need support from others – all of us do. While therapy is perhaps the most obvious example of this labour of emotional support, I am mainly interested in the unseen everyday effort that goes into keeping most of us relatively emotionally healthy, and maybe even happy.

We work under conditions not of our own choosing. Most people have to work in order to meet their own needs and the needs of the people they are close to. Our working conditions are not the result of individual agency but rather stem from the social organisation of production and reproduction – a system in which people's needs are met within various relations of power. These needs are partly grounded in the biological life of human organisms, such as our need for food and shelter. But they can only be met in historically specific ways, which are also determined by our social position. For example, our need for shelter can be met by a tent or a suburban one-family house. The constitution of various ways to meet our needs also gives rise to new needs. The growth of the suburbs, for instance, also created a need for cars to take people to and from their workplaces. What constitutes a need varies according to the classed, racialised, and gendered assignment of people to various categories in society. This book explores the construction of emotional needs and the material and subjective organisation of the labour that is necessary to meet them.

Women have been made largely responsible for the work of creating good feeling. In the past few years, there has been a revived interest in Marxist feminist thought and issues of social reproduction in both academia and activist groups. Marxism posits that capitalist society is characterised by the exploitation of the working class, whose work produces more value for the capitalist class than they receive back in the form of wages. Marxist feminism expands this understanding of capitalism to include that which has been coded as women's work – often done for free and out of love. With the recent revival of these theories, reproduction is being rediscovered as a central terrain of anti-capitalist struggle. Taking up the legacy of Marxist feminist writings from the late 1960s to the early 1980s, this new wave of research and organising aims to bring theories of reproductive labour into debates on the contemporary organisation of work. This means looking beyond women's unwaged domestic labour, the focus of much of the theoretical writings from the 1970s, to include various forms of waged employment in the reproductive sphere, such as childcare, nursing, and waged domestic labour.

Reproduction is an expansive field that contains the totality of the activities that sustain the lives of people under capitalism and maintain their capacity to work. Reproduction occupies a contradictory position in capitalist economies. It is necessary for the continued functioning of capitalist value production yet simultaneously devalued; geared towards the preservation of people's capacity to labour yet often excluded from the waged workplace and the formal economy. It spans people's unwaged work in their homes, commodified services, and some types of work associated with the public sector.

Across these very different parts of the landscape of contemporary capitalism, people are working, with or without a wage, to ensure the relative wellbeing of other people.

The capitalist economy is dependent on people doing this work of caring for each other either for free or for the low wages associated with reproductive service work. This work is often understood as unskilled, naturally feminine, and therefore a woman's duty, which should be carried out with little or no monetary reward. As Sarah Jaffe writes, 'Our willingness to accede that women's work is love, that love is its own reward, not to be sullied with money, creates profit for capital.'[1] Love's work is often relegated to the so-called private sphere of the home, and thus it is disavowed in modern political discourses. While incredibly common and mundane as a type of work, this activity has often been made invisible in economic and political analysis, including Marxist writings and organising. The task of the Marxist feminist tradition is to make this work visible in order to struggle against its current organisation. Decades of feminist writing and agitation have begun to undo some of the privatisation of reproduction – the process through which reproductive labour becomes an individual responsibility relegated to the private sphere. A shift in capitalist economies meant that much of reproduction now takes place outside the home. But reproduction is still understood as primarily the responsibility of the family, a social unit seen as the opposite of the capitalist sphere of work – our haven in a heartless world. Such privatisation of the burden and cost of reproductive work as well as the construction of a low-waged service economy serve to maintain women's subordinate position in a supposedly postfeminist era in which most legal constraints on women's independent existence have been removed. The privatisation of care makes women responsible for the wellbeing of others and undermines their financial and material independence while simultaneously constructing them as the people most suitable for this work and perpetuating the existence of a gendered division of labour.

Emotional reproduction includes the forms of work that go into maintaining people's emotional wellbeing and their ability and willingness to continue to engage in capitalist productive labour, often despite the considerable emotional strain produced by this work. Thinking about emotion across waged and unwaged sectors, I want to emphasise the work that goes into sustaining some degree of emotional wellbeing in people, such as comforting a loved one or making small talk with a lonely relative. Emotional reproduction is a broad term which denotes the work of creating not only certain feelings but the desires, needs, subjectivities, and forms of sociality that are both cause and effect of such labour. It is the formation of specific needs and the ways in which those needs are satisfied. Emotional reproduction creates a feeling of investment in the world as it is. We have emotional attachments to a particular notion of the good life – a normative way of life which seems to promise comfort and happiness. Our lives under capitalism are in many ways disappointing and continually create negative feelings such as stress, resentment, depression, and loneliness. But we all have an attachment to particular ideas of what a good life should look like – one that often includes the very sources of harm. We often continue to aspire to these ideals of the good life, even when they continually let us down.

When thinking about emotional reproduction, I draw on the concept of emotional labour, a term coined by sociologist Arlie Russell Hochschild in her 1983 book *The Managed Heart: Commercialization of Human Feeling*. Hochschild traces a shift in capitalist economies in which the growing service economy relies on the increased commodification of our emotional capacities. Commodification is the process through which an object or a service becomes something that can be bought and sold on the market. Hochschild's theory is based on a study of flight attendants, a traditionally feminised profession that involves not only serving food and drinks but also creating a sense of safety and emotional comfort in airline passengers. Feminised forms of emotional labour are oriented towards 'affirming, enhancing, and celebrating the wellbeing and status of others'.[2] From the example of flight attendants, Hochschild draws out a theory of the importance of emotion across a number of service jobs which are increasingly central in capitalist economies in Europe and North America.

Emotional labour has been commodified – it has been turned into a service that can be bought and sold. Following Hochschild, a number of researchers have studied the commodification of emotional labour in contemporary capitalism. But rather than seeing emotional labour as a phenomenon emerging with the growing service economy, I trace a longer history of emotional reproduction as part of both waged and unwaged forms of reproductive labour. The commodification of emotional labour has made such labour more visible, but it did not create it. By using the concept of emotional reproduction, I want to point to a broader process than the one usually described in sociological studies of emotional labour and include activities that would normally not be considered work. These activities may none-theless contribute to the emotional wellbeing of people, and should be politicised within the framework of reproduction. Like social reproduction more broadly, emotional reproduction operates across spheres of unwaged and waged work.

The point of this book is not to deny the need for emotional reproduction or call for its complete rejection. It is not a call to abandon forms of labour associated with femininity, or to grant women access to more masculine types of subjectivity. Fully rejecting the feminised work of care would be both impossible and undesirable. Rather, refusal of emotional reproduction refers to a mode of resistance that goes beyond the binary construction of gendered subjectivity, seeking to repurpose emotions, needs, and desires in order to find new ways of being together. This form of refusal might draw on

xiv

potentials existing in the present, including aspects of traditionally feminine subjectivity, but in ways that do not support the reproduction of the present.

This relies on the denaturalisation of femininity – regarding it as an acquired capacity rather than something inherent in particular subjects. In this way, we can also begin to consider emotion not as a merely spontaneous or natural state but as a type of skilful work. The concept of emotional labour helps us rethink both emotion, often regarded as passive, and labour, which tends to be constructed as conscious activity. Emotion is not a passive psychological state. But neither must something be fully conscious or active for it to be usefully considered as labour. To labour is to *do* something, but that something might not always be recognisable as activity. And while what we may legitimately call labour might always involve a product of some kind, this product will not always be recognisable as a 'thing' separate from its producer. Emotional labour is difficult to think about since the better it is done, the more it appears as non-work, both for the labourer and for the recipient of emotional care. All labour may involve effort on the side of the labourer, yet such exertion might appear as merely a natural expression of the labouring subject. In emotional labour processes in particular, the result of the work is often invisible as a product and comes to appear as an aspect of the personality of the worker. As Sophie Lewis argues, in these forms of labour, 'a feminized person's body is typically being further feminized: it is working very, very hard at having the appearance of not working at all'.[3] Our labour practices therefore become aspects of what we experience as our authentic selves. In its seeming passivity, emotional labour is similar to other feminised forms of work. It is ironic that the labour associated with femininity is often seen as passive and that femininity is associated with receptivity, as women do much of the work of reproducing people.

Some of the discomfort with the term emotional labour, as well as its popularity inside and outside academic discourse, probably stems from this seeming conceptual mismatch between emotion and labour. The concept's impropriety makes it both expansive and confusing, placing all sorts of phenomena under its banner. But this expansiveness is part of the nature of emotional labour, and it is important to theorise it despite its elusiveness. Otherwise, we leave emotion unexamined, falling back on more common-sense notions of emotion as natural, intimate, non-social, and spontaneous.

I want to situate emotional labour within Marxist feminist theories of reproduction, in particular the theory and strategy developed by the Wages for Housework movement. Wages for Housework was founded in 1972 by a group of Italian, British, French, and American feminists, and their activism sought to highlight all the work that goes into caring for people – work primarily done by women. I draw on the theoretical contributions by Wages for Housework writers such as Silvia Federici, Mariarosa Dalla Costa, Giovanna Franca Dalla Costa, Leopoldina Fortunati, Wilmette Brown, Ruth Hall, and Selma James. Their writings emphasised the essential character of housework, and reproductive work more broadly, to the smooth functioning of capitalist societies. The Wages for Housework writers and activists asserted that the sphere of reproduction is politically important and that the people engaged in this work occupy a central position in anti-capitalist struggles. They described this work as both indispensable to the reproduction of capital and a potential site of its disruption. The central demand of the movement was for the capitalist state to pay a wage for currently unwaged or low-waged forms of reproductive labour. In this way, they hoped to show that capitalism cannot be profitable if all reproductive work is paid. Their analysis started from the position of working-class housewives in European and North American countries, but it included a range of people who perform some form of reproductive labour – waitresses, sex workers, nannies, secretaries, and other feminised workers. They also paid attention to the interconnections of gender, race, class, and sexuality in the sphere of reproduction. Wages Due Lesbians and Black Women for Wages for Housework were autonomous groups organising as part of the Wages for Housework movement, which contributed to an integrated analysis of different forms of exploitation and oppression under capitalism.

Since the prime of 1970s Marxist feminism, women's economic and social position has changed. After the post-war period ended, the status of women's labour has shifted, as has the notion of 'women' as a collective subject. I use the term neoliberalism to capture the current political moment, where states and capital have sought to deregulate labour markets and privatise previously state-owned resources and institutions. A decline in real wages led to dual-income families and women's increased participation in waged labour. Neoliberalism also brought with it a shift to a service economy. Before this, in the post-war period, European and North American capitalism was still oriented around industrial production, and reproductive labour mostly took place in the home. This periodisation can easily become too simplified, and the term neoliberalism has been used to describe all kinds of phenomena. But there are significant differences between women's position before the mid-1970s and their position today. The writings of the Wages for Housework movement, and other Marxist feminist texts and movements from the same period, were seeking to intervene in feminist and leftist debates of the 1970s – a time when many working-age women were housewives. They therefore cannot fully account for women's position in the labour market today. However, there are also important continuities between what is labelled as women's work, even as more of it has become integrated into the low-waged service sector. Women still perform significant amounts of unwaged care work, and they are more likely than men to be employed in reproductive sectors. I draw on the Wages for Housework writings to understand those continuities.

The emotional and subjective aspects of reproductive labour are central to the disruptive potential of this work. Emotional reproduction is tied to the reproduction of gender difference, but could it be mobilised to create a collective feminist subjectivity? I want to locate possible sites of struggle within the sphere of social reproduction and create a theory informed by the needs of political struggle aimed at constituting and enhancing antagonism between the exploiters and the exploited. Silvia Federici, a co-founder of Wages for Housework, uses the term 'struggle concepts' – that is, concepts that name and produce antagonistic relations.[4] Emotional reproduction is a struggle concept through which we can view our emotional lives as inherently political.

Feeling Work

The term emotional reproduction describes how emotion participates in the continual remaking of the world. This remaking is tied to hierarchical forms of labour and reward but could potentially be turned into a project of making the world differently. The world as we know it is marked by disparities in which some people experience a lack of emotional comfort, leading to perennial loneliness and poor mental health. Other people experience an excess of emotional comfort, as they are shielded from experiencing other people's distress and emotional depletion. The current organisation of labour is ultimately detrimental to the emotional wellbeing of most people. Like reproduction more broadly, emotional reproduction is seriously constrained by capitalist imperatives to produce value, as well as by structures such as racism, sexism, and homophobia. Emotional reproduction is currently based on exploited labour within families and a lack of attention to the emotional needs of those who are excluded from family bonds. Improving the emotional lives of the majority thus depends on the radical transformation of emotional reproduction.

Those who appear to be the independent subjects of the labour contract, selling their capacities on the free market, are in fact dependent on others for the maintenance of their ability to labour. Historically, inhabiting this form of subjectivity has been the privilege of white men, whereas children, housewives, slaves, and colonial subjects have been excluded from the ability to sell their own labour power. Today, women in European and North American countries are almost as active in the formal labour force as men, either from a desire to leave the domestic sphere or by the whip of economic need. Through equality feminisms and the neoliberal reconstitution of reproduction, some women have been granted an (always precarious and partial) access to the subjectivity of possessive individualism – an understanding of the self that posits that the subject is the sovereign proprietor of its own capacities, owing nothing to society for them. This does not mean that gender hierarchy has been overcome, or that the need for housework within the family has been fully replaced by market-provided services. Some of the work previously associated with the role of the housewife has undergone a partial and fragmentary reshuffling. However, it is still the case that those who appear as sovereign subjects (primarily white men, and increasingly some white bourgeois women) most often have their needs quietly met by others, who are seen as less-free subjects because of their association with the devalued labour of reproduction.

The work of producing emotional wellbeing shows how reproduction is intimately connected to modes of subjectivity, as emotional labourers work on the subjectivities of others as well as on their own. The hegemonic form of subjectivity in capitalism – possessive individualism – simultaneously disavows and depends on a feminised subjectivity of care. A radical politics of emotional reproduction is one which seeks to undo these gendered forms of subjectivity. This calls for the abolition of the nuclear family as a primary site of heterosexualised emotional reproduction, which excludes the queer and racialised forms of reproduction that function as the constitutive outside of the normative family form. While familial and romantic ideals of love serve to reproduce some people and some types of life, they simultaneously make others vulnerable to violence and neglect, and exclude them from access to reproductive resources such as housing and healthcare. Moving beyond the family as the dominant form of sociality can open up space for new ways of being together and reproducing each other.

This struggle relies on an antiwork perspective. Antiwork theory and organising takes aim at the central position that work has within our lives, not just to create better conditions of work, but to struggle against a system that forces us to give up all our time to working for others. A feminist antiwork perspective criticises the current organisation of labour across waged and unwaged spheres. Going beyond the orthodox Marxist critique of the exploitation of industrial labour through the employment contract, it emphasises the capitalist reliance on reproductive labour across market, state, and domestic spheres.

The aim of a feminist movement against the capitalist organisation of reproduction should be to make certain activities, which we today must describe as work, into non-work or antiwork. I use the concept of work to describe processes that are unfree or involuntary, in the sense that we are compelled to do them in order to satisfy our needs and those of other people. This means that these processes could potentially become non-work if they are disconnected from the conditions that compel us to perform them. The same activity might be work for one person but play or a hobby for someone else, depending on the circumstances. For example, hunting or sewing might be work for the hunter or tailor but a leisure activity for other people. The term work should be understood as a shifting, unstable political category which is best characterised through the link between certain activities and the imperative to satisfy one's needs and the needs of others. Viewed in this way, there is nothing that inherently makes an activity work or non-work, and what we regard as work is open to contestation and struggle. Intimate activities such as sex and emotional expressions of love can become work through their coercive connection to the sphere of capitalist reproduction. This also means that they could become non-work if freed from the forms of constraint that characterise such reproduction. Such liberation would not take love and sex as given, transhistorical things but drastically change them so that they might not be recognisable as the same phenomena. Queer and otherwise marginalised communities are showing the way towards more playful and liberatory potentials for emotion and desire. This might involve re-imagining and repurposing supposedly bad feelings along the way.

This perspective implies using the concept of work in such a way as to loosen work's power over our lives and capacities. In recognising that there is nothing inevitable in the current organisation of work, and in our current capabilities, we can move towards exploring other modes of being as well as confronting the organisation of the world that has turned certain activities into labour. Labour is something we do to meet our needs and those of others, not something that expresses our authentic selves. If work as a concept indicates a non-voluntary aspect of activities usually taken to be natural expressions of gendered personality, it is also something that can be resisted, rethought, and abolished, as our needs and desires could be met differently.

Federici writes that 'you work, not because you like it, or because it comes naturally to you, but because it is the only condition under which you are allowed to live. Exploited as you might be, you are not that work.'[5] Recently, Lewis has theorised pregnancy as work, thus challenging the notion that work must include conscious, mental activity, as well as the notion that pregnancy is a passive, natural capacity of the body. Quoting Maggie Nelson's description of the work of giving birth, Lewis states: 'You don't do labor. Labor does you.'[6] Here, the notion of the individual subject's autonomy is radically subverted in a way we might usefully embrace. Employing the term work to describe these processes is a way of creating a gap between what we are and what we could be. If labour does you, but you are not that work, then who we could be is a radically open question. As Federici writes, 'We want to call work what is work so that eventually we might rediscover what is love and create our sexuality, which we have never known.'[7] Marxist feminism is an essential tool for saying that we could be more than our labour.

This move to abolish work, and therefore current forms of subjectivity, might entail questioning our sense of pleasure in our work and our gendered being. While gendered performance and emotional labour can be pleasurable, this does not mean that they are not exploitative. In particular, the pleasures that people derive from heterosexuality and familial love need to be questioned in this context, both because they are built on the exploitation of feminised people and because of the exclusions and limitations such pleasurable reproduction creates. The point, then, is not so much about what types of work people do or do not enjoy, but about what kinds of subjects work turns us into. Certain types of labour might require a high degree of subjective investment from labourers. Such investments, however, also delimit what we could be and the types of pleasure available to us. The kind of gender/work abolition that I propose takes subjective investments and pleasures into account, but also asks what we could be if we were not forced to make that kind of subjective investment in exploitative structures. We should assume that there could be other, better pleasures.

Labour is simultaneously productive and repressive. It demarcates subjective possibilities according to a division of labour – a process through which subjects come into being. The skilled performance of certain types of work constitutes subjectivities but also limits the possibilities of other subjects who are not determined by normative forms of labour. The creation of a labouring subject is not a mere reduction of human capacities, but constitutes and channels capacities in a particular direction. This serves to impoverish our ability to feel and act in ways that are not supported by the dominant organisation of labour. The abolition of gender involves the unlearning of some of our acquired capacities for emotion so that other capacities can be developed. Such un- or relearning is part and parcel of political interventions into the organisations of social and material life. The potential for this relearning, however, should not be located in notions of an eternal human nature. There is no underlying, truer form of subjectivity that we can discover once we cast off capitalist forms of being. Rather, potentials for resistance can emerge as by-products of the organisation of labour. Resistance arises from other forms of needs and pleasures which are not satisfied with the world as it is. Labour creates the immanent possibilities of its own refusal. From these possibilities, a queer reproduction can emerge based on the practices, needs, and pleasures of those currently most marginalised by hegemonic notions of the good life.

1

Emotional Reproduction

The family is often reported to be 'in crisis', and people appear to be increasingly atomised and isolated. Yet family relationships remain emotionally charged, even as family is seemingly less central in our lives. This is because capitalism prevents many other forms of sociality. While capitalism is sometimes understood as a system leading to increasingly fleeting and meaningless social encounters, bourgeois society has in fact brought with it a culture in which emotion is paramount, but where only a few key relationships become crucial for one's emotional life. The family remains the 'proper' place of intense feeling, and the most important source of emotional wellbeing, but it also continually produces pain, trauma, and disappointment, as well as investment in ideologies of love and labour.

It is mostly through intimate relationships that we reproduce ourselves emotionally, and that we create our sense of authentic subjectivity. But these relationships are often in themselves a source of pain and frustration. They routinely fail to live up to what Sara Ahmed calls 'the promise of happiness' – the idea that certain life paths will ensure good feeling.[1] Romantic relationships, supposedly one of the most important ways to achieve emotional satisfaction, often cause distress and bad feelings. Yet we keep hoping that one day, if we just find the right person, we will have satisfying romantic lives – a true love that will last forever. Love has had a central position in modern and contemporary ideals of the good life. Not finding love is often experienced as a failure and a sign of personal lack. For women especially, romance is equated with personal worth.

The family itself, as an ideal form of sociality, remains at the heart of what we think of as the good life. We hope that if we can just build a family of our own, we will finally be happy.

These emotional investments in a particular form of sociality, as well as the labour that goes into creating good feelings within those relationships, is what I call emotional reproduction. Emotional reproduction is not only a form of labour; it is also a system of social relations and ideologies which form the framework for where and how that labour takes place. Emotional reproduction is both cause and effect of our emotional investment in the ideology of family and romance. The term highlights the essential nature of emotional labour for the reproduction of labour power and capitalist social relations. While emotional labour is a specific type of labour, it cannot be understood outside the context of reproductive labour more broadly. Emotional reproduction today spans the divisions between public and private spheres and waged and unwaged work. But I am particularly interested in the intimate work of producing emotional satisfaction within family and romantic relationships.

Emotion is elusive. It is not an object which we can easily identify and separate from other phenomena. Rather, in Alison Jaggar's words, it describes a form of habit or a way of engaging with the world which escapes simple dichotomies of activity and passivity. Emotions presume language and social order, and they are closely linked to social values and modes of evaluation.[2] Emotions such as anger or shame imply a social judgement of some kind, as do feelings of happiness and attachment. These social values have to be learnt. Feelings are rule-bound processes – they are not spontaneous eruptions but rather profoundly social phenomena which are learnt and managed by the subject. While often understood as something internal, a psychological state within the subject, emotion signals the subject's involvement with the world.[3] Emotions are not passive states that we simply endure, but neither are they things a subject can fully control or will into being. They form part of the very constitution of the subject itself, and are fundamental to constituting the subject as a social being. Emotion, then, should be conceptualised not as coming from within the subject, but rather as a form of interaction between the subject and the social, through which the subject becomes involved in the social world. This includes relations of power, which can become internalised through emotional processes. We learn to feel that existing power relations are natural and good, and that social change is wrong, unnatural, and frightening.

We often think of capitalism as a system devoid of feeling – driven either by rationality or hunger for profit, depending on our perspective. But this understanding of capitalism cannot account for the gendered work of producing good feeling. Capitalism depends on emotional reproduction. Emotion and sociality form crucial aspects of how we stay alive and sometimes even thrive. Workers often cannot expect emotional wellbeing or satisfaction from their own work, but emotional reproduction seeks to make up for the hurt, boredom, and stress of life under capitalism.

I use the term emotional labour to mean interactive work that produces emotional effects in another person. This work includes constituting and reproducing emotional bonds. Emotional labour always impacts the labouring subject as well as the recipient of emotional labour – for example, these subjects reproduce gendered identities through the relation of labour. There is therefore a connection between emotional management of the self and that of others. Emotion is a process in which acts of expressing, suppressing, and shaping feeling have to be constantly repeated and managed and are bound to the construction of particular forms of subjectivity. The term emotional labour, then, describes this work of managing the emotions of oneself and others.

Emotional labour is often presented as the opposite of our genuine and authentic selves. There is a tendency in the literature on emotional labour to take something like a 'real' or non-managed feeling as the ideal. But while subjective interiority appears as given and natural, we do not need to rely on notions of authentic subjectivity in order to critique emotional labour. As Kathi Weeks suggests, labour practices have an ontologising effect – they make a subject come into being. The subject comes to appear as a stable entity through memory, desire, and habit.[4] These things become interiorised through skilful repetitions of certain forms of work. The subject comes to experience its socially constituted self as authentic and pre-social. This is especially the case for emotional labour.

A focus on the link between emotion management of the self and the management of other people's emotions shows how emotion is not only cognitive and immaterial but also part of embodied practice. As Arlie Russell Hochschild writes, emotional labour involves a 'publicly observable facial and bodily display'.[5] But emotional labour is embodied not only in the sense of using the body as a tool for communicating emotion, but also because emotion itself involves bodily as well as cognitive dispositions. It is not only a mental practice; it is something that involves the body. We feel emotions in our bodies – from the tension of anger or anxiety to the warmth of joy. This challenges modern dichotomies of body and mind, as well as those of activity and passivity.

We often understand our feelings as expressions of an inner truth. But the subject experiencing emotion need not be understood as a pre-social or authentic self. Instead, this subject should be seen within a specific historical context and as produced by particular processes of labour. The conventional, rule-bound aspects of emotion can tell us something about the historical constitution of the subject of emotional labour. Raymond Williams's phrase 'structure of feeling' reminds us that feeling is not random or spontaneous but tied to various historical processes. As Williams writes, structures of feeling are not recognised as such; instead, they are 'taken to be private, idiosyncratic, and even isolating, but which in analysis . . . has its emergent, connecting, and dominant characteristics, indeed its specific hierarchies'.[6] There is no need to posit emotion as the source of our core identity. We use emotion to locate our supposedly authentic selves, but emotion is subjected to various forms of management. Hochschild writes that 'we make up an idea of our "real self", an inner jewel that remains our unique possession'.[7] Our authentic selves are themselves the result of historically specific practices, including labour processes.

Emotion has an important role to play in shoring up our sense of identity and subjectivity. Subjectivity under capitalism is fundamentally bound to hierarchy. The notion of a coherent subject who is the master of his own capacities is tied to various forms of material and social inequality, as this form of subjectivity is more available to bourgeois white men. However, these inequalities become invisible in the making of the sovereign subject, as it depends precisely on the erasure of the social. Emotional reproduction is central in the production of both subjectivity and status – through responsibility for producing emotional wellbeing, what forms of subjectivity result from those labour practices, and what emotions are deemed appropriate and rational.

The subject as we know it is the result of a historical process related to changes in social relations at the inception of capitalism. As Cinzia Arruzza puts it, 'A robust notion of the privacy of affects as characterizing what it means to be a unique individual arises with capitalism and modernity.'[8] Historian Lawrence Stone calls this 'affective individualism' – the idea of an individual with a private and affective interior life, which focuses on the individual's emotional self-expression.[9] In the medieval period, the self was conceptualised as 'far less contained, privatized and controlled' than it is today.[10] The notion of the emotionally bounded individual is tied to capitalist-colonial systems of power as well as gendered forms of labour.[11] Social relations of power and hierarchy are therefore implicit in our intimate understandings of ourselves. The fact that many modern theorists have criticised this notion of a coherent, sovereign subject has not led to its disappearance, because we cannot simply do away with this understanding of the self intellectually – it is implicated in real social relations of capitalism, in particular ones related to gender, race, and labour.

According to Arruzza, our sense of ourselves as ontologically pre-given subjects exists in contradiction with another process in capitalist society, in which emotions come to appear as things detachable from their subjects and separate from their social context.[12] This is part of a general process of the commodification of things and services. This means that two seemingly contradictory developments – the understanding of the self as authentic and pre-social and the view that emotions are detachable from the subject – are both part of a modern, capitalist understanding of the subject.[13] This process is particularly noticeable in commodified forms of emotional labour which draw on supposedly intimate feelings in ways that people might experience as alienating. Our ability to smile and create a warm and caring atmosphere becomes a thing that can be sold on the labour market. We can understand this conflict between the real self and reified emotion as an interiorised version of the dichotomy between private and public in capitalist society. This dichotomy is historically constructed and unstable, but it produces real social effects. Subjective interiority is constructed through a process in which emotions become expressions of an authentic self while simultaneously emerging as highly malleable material for labour – feelings we can work on, manage, and control.

Love as Labour

The primary function of emotional labour is to create good feeling. For most companies that provide emotional services as

6

part of their product, as well as for much unwaged emotional labour, the aim is to increase the emotional wellbeing of at least one of the participants. Emotional labour is a form of care which is often an integral part of more physical types of care. Caring practices can involve various degrees of emotional labour. Hochschild's flight attendants perform a particular form of care, where smiling and comforting passengers are primary functions of the job. In some cases, care can involve less emotional labour, as the main aim is to satisfy physical need. Sometimes, physical care can be accompanied with emotional neglect or even abuse. We cannot take for granted that caring labour will necessarily work across both physical and emotional levels. Emotional labour is a semi-autonomous aspect of social reproduction more broadly. But the satisfaction of physical needs, such as the need for food, often contains an emotional component. Making food that will suit the individual preferences of the person being cared for, for example, can become a sign of emotional attachment to that person.[14] As Anne Boyer puts it, the face that says 'love me' often means something like 'bring me some soup'.[15] But the act of bringing someone soup can also be a way of saying 'I love you'. Because this work is so intimate, and tailored to individual need, it is often impossible to separate the emotional side of reproduction from the physical tasks. Much emotional care takes place through various physical acts of care. While some forms of work require more obvious forms of emotional labour, even the work of flight attendants includes tasks such as providing food and drink.

Emotional reproduction can work as a kind of organising principle of care, as caring about someone is in many cases an aspect of caring for that person. The intimate labour of care often results in emotional involvement, although that involvement might not consist of positive emotions such as love or empathy but can also cause emotions such as disgust, boredom, or anger. Emotional labour can involve the management and suppression of these negative emotions as much as it can foster feelings of love or affection. This is also part of the creation of good feeling.

Through ongoing caring practices, disparate acts are integrated into an emotional bond. Care most often involves a multitude of different tasks, some of which might be invisible because they consist of the mental work that goes into coordinating the satisfaction of various needs. In some cases, white bourgeois wives and mothers are seen as performing the labour of love even when they delegate many of the practical aspects of that work to domestic workers. Because of the emotional bond between the wife/mother and her husband and children, emotional labour might become more visible when she performs it, while also being more naturalised. The labour of nannies and domestic workers is usually written out of the story of the good life.

Emotional labour tends to cater to those at the top of the social hierarchy, as the feelings of those with higher status are often granted greater importance than the feelings of subordinated people. This is especially true of the creation of positive feeling, which, as Hochschild argues, tends to move upwards in social hierarchies. As she puts it, subordinates generally 'owe' more emotional labour than dominant partners in relationships.[16] Within the heterosexual family, women are expected to contribute more to the continued emotional well-being of individual family members as well as ensure the maintenance of the family bond itself.[17] They are asked to put the emotional needs of others ahead of their own or, even better, make the fulfilment of the needs of others the cause of their own happiness. This is reproduced in many service jobs, where the enjoyment of caring for others becomes a precondition for doing the job well. Emotional reproduction is also the reproduction of social hierarchy, where those who are already comfortable have their needs met to a much greater extent than those at the bottom of the social hierarchy.

Part of the work of emotional reproduction is producing ideological investment. This is reproduction in the sense of continually recreating an attachment to the world as we know it. Ideology depends on such emotional investment – it is not just a mental belief but a way of feeling and relating to the world. Ideology would not *stick* without feeling. To some degree, ideology is feeling. It is through emotional reproduction that we come to invest emotionally in the right objects and the right futures. Through the privatisation of emotional reproduction, bad feeling becomes individualised. Emotional reproduction serves to smooth over malcontent with the dominant order, creating a belief that we can and should have satisfying emotional lives under capitalism. Emotional reproduction naturalises the world as it is and makes it appear as a desirable state of things – as long as we make the right choices and behave in the right way. If we are unhappy, we just need to manage our feelings better.

The ideology of romance tells us we could be happy if we could just find true love. Under capitalism, love is a highly privatised resource. Love is seen as an intensive emotion but also something that is restricted to a limited sphere. This is related to a conception of emotion as a zero-sum game in which emotional bonds owe their intensity to their exclusivity. Stone argues that affective individualism brought with it a notion of the subject who had a heightened affective capacity but for a more restrictive group of people.[18] These intense emotional relationships also involve heightened emotional expectations. We are supposed to be able to meet all the emotional needs of those we love. Intimate relationships contain a potentially infinite number of tasks, as they are intended to respond to individualised and unique needs.[19] This means that emotional labour, and reproductive labour more broadly, is not experienced as a limited set of tasks that can be ticked off on a list. Rather, our contemporary understanding of loving relationships requires them to be without measure.[20] But this supposedly infinite and unconditional nature of love does not lead to an equal division of love's labour. For women, this understanding of love entails an expectation of being constantly available to meet the emotional needs of people they love. Love's work is never done, and you can always do more to show your affection. The difficulty of measuring emotional labour, a challenge for those who seek to commodify it, has always been an integral and crucial aspect of this work, especially when it is performed unwaged and out of love. It becomes a way of extracting an unlimited amount of reproductive labour.

As the material acts of reproduction often operate through emotional bonds, and are co-constitutive with them, it is difficult to fully separate reproductive labour from emotional labour. As Giovanna Franca Dalla Costa writes, love is seen as a reward for reproductive labour, and what makes this work sufferable.[21] It is also a feeling that hides the effort and skill that goes into caring. While not all relationships based on care work or emotional labour involve feelings of love, it is an organising principle of many of our most important and enduring reproductive relationships. Other forms of care are constructed as being worthy or good work and therefore inherently rewarding. The work of nurses involves many of the same emotional structures that bind people to their unwaged work in the home.[22] But we tend to understand our intimate relationships as more genuine – as expressions of our true feelings.

Hochschild notes that intimate relationships are supposedly free from regulation, consisting merely of the spontaneous expression of love. But the work of regulating our emotions according to certain social rules may be more important the deeper the relationship, owing to our heightened attachment to those relationships.[23] While a breach of the rules of emotional exchange in an ephemeral service encounter might not generate anything more than annoyance, emotional neglect in an intimate relationship might be experienced as a threat to the subject itself. As Laurent Berlant puts it, intimate attachments are central to 'the continuity of the subject's sense of what it means to keep on living and to look forward to being in the world'.[24] The narrative of the good life becomes intimately bound up with the subject's own selfhood.

In modernity, love has become what confirms the value of a person, especially in the intimate sphere of reproduction.[25] More specifically, love entails focusing on the desirable qualities of the other, and attending to their specificity and uniqueness.[26] Emotional reproduction often ensures that not only do acts of reproductive labour serve to satisfy the needs of individuals, they can also affirm the status of the recipient of care as a unique individual. It therefore participates in the construction of individualism. This can include seemingly insignificant acts of reproductive labour, such as cooking a meal in a way that attends to the specific preferences of family members.[27] It can also include acts that affirm your partner's status or gendered subjectivity – their sense of themselves as a 'real' man or woman.[28] All these acts contribute to the emotional evaluation of an individual, as well as ensure that their basic needs are met. Needs become an expression of individualism, as these needs are seen as a form of unique self-expression.

As Sophie Lewis points out, just because something is work does not mean it is not love.[29] The point is precisely the entanglement of work and feeling. Love places limits on the refusal of emotional and reproductive labour – as Dalla Costa writes, it can be difficult to stage a slowdown or a strike when it affects loved ones.[30] Love can thus be used to extract an ongoing, infinite amount of labour – a work relationship that may stretch over a whole lifetime. Feminist writings on care often mention the feeling of guilt as a corollary of love.[31] Even though it is a negative emotion, one that people try to avoid, it is closely connected to love. Hochschild notes that we can feel guilty for failing to feel the right thing, or for feeling what is owed to the other.[32] Guilt tethers people to intimate work relations, ensuring that the work owed in that relationship is carried out. Guilt can be a threat to one's sense of self as a

generous, loving person, and thus undermine a positive evaluation of the self.[33] However, it can also reinforce that sense of
self – the feeling of guilt can act as an indication that one is
actually a good person, even when one fails to do good things.
Most forms of emotional labour make the subject understand
itself as emotionally generous and giving. Silvia Federici notes
that emotional investment in the object of caring work can
entail emotions of responsibility and pride, thus preventing
the worker from cutting those attachments, even when they
are exploitative.[34] This is the case especially in intimate relationships, where the emotional cost of not doing what is owed
often becomes too much to bear.

Many people do leave relationships that are emotionally
unsatisfactory, and changed emotional expectations over the
past decades have made divorce more socially acceptable. But
aside from the economic precarity many people experience,
which often makes it difficult to break up family relationships,
emotional investment can serve to maintain ongoing intimate
work relationships, even when they are emotionally unsatisfactory. According to bourgeois ideology, emotional needs can
only be fully satisfied within the family, which might make it
seem risky to opt out of even unfulfilling family arrangements.
The family has monopolised care in a way that makes it more
difficult to build alternative forms of caring relationships.[35] As
Hochschild notes, persistent gender inequality deepens women's
emotional debt, thus making it more difficult not to fulfil family
obligations. Even in supposedly egalitarian heterosexual couples,
the wider context of gender inequality posits that women owe
men gratitude for such relative equality.[36] This situation fixes
standards for emotional exchange while contributing to the
reproduction of gender within intimate relationships. Being
perceived as emotionally generous, and watching loved ones
flourish emotionally, is key to a feminised ideal of the good life.
Failing to have happy relationships, on the other hand, becomes
a sign of failing to be a good woman.

Parenting and Emotional Reproduction

Together with the ideology of romance, having children of your own is seen as a key source of emotional satisfaction, particularly for women. In contemporary capitalist society, children's emotional needs are often afforded great social importance. At the outset of the modern period, children were increasingly constructed as a different kind of being from adults.[37] Children are now seen as innocent and unsullied by the supposedly cold and unfeeling logic of capitalism.[38] As Viviana Zelizer writes, because children are no longer expected to work and contribute to the family income, they are increasingly seen as economically worthless but emotionally priceless.[39] Childhood is constructed as a period of emotional intensity, and mothers especially are made responsible for meeting the varying emotional needs of their children. In the modern period, there has been a shift in parenting methods, as physical discipline was de-emphasised at the same time as love came to appear as the primary tool for socialising children. Displays of parental love could be used to reward children, and withdrawal of these displays became the primary means for punishing a child for bad behaviour.[40] Love has become a disciplinary force.

This shift coincided with the rise of psychological experiments around childhood attachment as well as literature aimed at mothers which emphasised the need for a primary caregiver.[41] Children's emotional needs were thus constructed in a way that meant only one person could satisfy them. Even with the rise of 'working mothers' and daycare centres, where more people were involved in childcare, this notion of individualised parenting was retained or even intensified. Mothers are constructed as primary parents – the people responsible for fulfilling their children's need for emotional warmth.[42] Motherhood is also presented as an emotionally unique experience, which means that mothers are seen as having a uniquely intense bond with their children. Emotional need is privatised in the sense that it is tied to a specific person and cannot be fulfilled in the same way by someone else. Emotional reproduction emerges as a zero-sum game, in which emotional satisfaction is linked to exclusive bonds. This type of mothering is labour-intensive and emotionally absorbing. While this standard for emotional reproduction is closely associated with the rise of bourgeois culture, it affects working-class mothering as well, as it is tied to notions of aspiration and class mobility.[43] This standard is also used for state regulation of working-class mothering, as these mothers are measured against the norms of what counts as 'good enough' mothering for the middle class and the bourgeoisie. This form of mothering is based on the contradiction whereby an increased focus on the subject's capacity for intense emotions is coupled with a notion of wider capitalist society as devoid of emotion or, at most, as treating emotion as a commodity.

The idea of feeling as a zero-sum game is based on a form of emotional privatisation. Within families, it is often mothers who are responsible for meeting family members' emotional needs. Mothers, Cameron Lynne Macdonald writes, are seen as having 'blanket accountability' for how their children turn out.[44] While often understood as the antithesis of capitalist rationality, motherhood is not separate from capitalism but an important aspect of setting the emotional standards in capitalist societies. Mothers are also assigned responsibility for constituting and maintaining the bonds between fathers and children, therefore having a responsibility not only for the emotional wellbeing of the child itself but for the emotional life of the family. Mothers are seen as love's experts, working to interpret the emotional needs of different members of the family so that the family might continue to exist.[45]

But the sphere of the family is not a site of natural emotional bonds. Emotional expectations for what a parent–child bond should entail are themselves situated within a wider social context which has changed drastically over the course of modern history. The emotional life of the family is not outside of the emotional regulation of waged work but rather co-constituted with these regulations and responsive to changes in the broader emotional standards of capitalism. Hochschild writes that parental love is constructed as 'natural' and unconditional, and therefore not in need of regulation. She writes that we think of this love as spontaneous, as nature supposedly 'does the work of convention for us'.[46] But these bonds do rely on emotional regulation and historically specific expectations of what constitutes good-enough mothering.

Emotional need is historically constituted and tied to specific forms of sociality which entail potentially exploitative forms of labour. This construction of need can also mean that mothers' emotional wellbeing is sacrificed for the sake of their children.[47] Mothers' own emotional needs then have to be adjusted so that they are satisfied through the emotional satisfaction of their family members. But if we start to disentangle those needs, we can see that they are often conflicting and cannot all be satisfied at the same time. Emotional need cannot be taken as a given, as there might be competing needs that cannot be satisfied. A care worker's need for rest might come into contradiction with another person's need for emotional comfort. This makes need a shaky foundation for radical politics – we cannot change society based simply on what people need.

The idea that children's emotional satisfaction must be prioritised over that of adults depends on a cultural zoning of childhood as a time of particular emotional intensity. The social construction of children as especially emotionally needy – and in need of the love of their primary carer – has long been used to extract more emotional and physical labour from mothers. Leopoldina Fortunati criticises the psychological literature aimed at mothers, which establishes those emotional standards by asserting that children who are not loved enough become 'maladjusted'.[48] This understanding of childcare makes women morally responsible for both the current and future wellbeing of the child. Emotional reproduction in childhood is constructed as the foundation of successful reproduction more broadly. Social problems are blamed on the supposed failure of women to love their children enough. Teresa Brennan emphasises the importance of emotional care through a reading of studies on the effects of a lack of love on orphaned children, which suggests that such children do not physically grow at an average rate. She uses this argument to undo the boundaries of the physical and the psychic, arguing that love itself is the basis of biological life and consciousness.[49] However, under current social relations, this is easily turned into a moralising argument which blames a lack of emotional and physical flourishing on individuals, most often mothers.

Emotional Class Reproduction

While we tend to associate reproductive work with the reproduction of people, class distinctions themselves need to be continually reproduced. The emotional conditioning of children is a fundamental aspect of reproducing capitalist class relations. Bourgeois mothering is responsive to the naturalised and individualised emotional needs of children, and therefore teaches them that those needs are important. Hochschild suggests that middle-class parents prime their children for high-status professions by focusing on developing a capacity for decision-making.[50] Middle- and upper-class parenting also involves encouraging children to experience themselves as affective individuals with their own unique emotional lives. This prepares children for success in their future careers, ensuring the preservation or improvement of the family's class advantage.[51] This model of parenting, in which families are seen as competing over scarce resources of upward mobility, serves to constantly increase the emotional standards of childhood. Parents are made to invest more and more time in the emotional guidance of children as well as pay for expensive services that will educate their child to be able to compete on the job market. Intensive mothering is a way of translating the logic of the market within the family.[52]

White bourgeois mothering in particular involves demands for 'spiritual' work. This includes moral guidance and education of the child's needs and desires. Dorothy Roberts writes that white women's bonds with their children are seen as unique and exclusive even when the children spend more time with a nanny or at daycare.[53] This stems from an understanding of femininity and family as our haven in the heartless world of capital. Sharon Hays writes that the nineteenth-century ideal of white bourgeois motherhood was centred around raising virtuous future citizens of the nation.[54] The bourgeois nation was also a white nation, linking the spiritual reproduction of children to racial ideals. In practical terms, this was related to a racial and classed division of labour within social reproduction, where black, brown, working-class, and immigrant women were relegated to menial tasks, whereas white bourgeois women took on the spiritual and emotional guidance of men and children.[55] This spiritual work has always been more highly valued. It contributes to the ambiguous status of motherhood, which is simultaneously devalued and glorified. The spiritual duty of mothers has been used as a way of claiming rights and status for white bourgeois women, as a reward for their work of raising virtuous citizens.[56] Emotional reproduction can be used to create hierarchies among women, as only some women were able to claim a position as the mothers and moral guides of the nation. Working-class and racialised women were left out of the glorified account of motherhood. These women supposedly do not perform the right kind of class transmission to ensure the reproduction of the white bourgeois nation. Their work is therefore seen as unskilled, and is subjected to various forms of control and stigma.

Hochschild argues that middle-class families have long trained their children for emotion management through stressing the importance of feelings. The child learns that their own emotions have a social importance, but also that they can be instrumentalised and adjusted.[57] This form of parenting has an appearance of freedom, as middle-class parenting centres on the needs and desires of the child. But those needs and desires are not given. Rather, they are created through the very process of parenting that is supposedly responding to them. Middle-class parenting, according to Hochschild, works not against but through the will of the child. The whole project of parenting is about educating that will in the right direction, and teaching the child to desire class reproduction. The child is taught to want the right kind of life – including a career, a house, and a family that is often very similar to what their parents themselves have or aspire to.

According to Hochschild, working-class parents are more likely to emphasise obedience and discipline.[58] She explains this by the fact that working-class people are more likely to work with things than with people, and therefore they do not need to learn skills of emotion management and social interaction in the same way as middle- and upper-class people. But since Hochschild wrote *The Managed Heart*, more and more working-class people are employed in service occupations characterised by strict regulation of emotional expression. The demand for the emotional style of discipline and deference remains central for working-class jobs. Working-class children may therefore need to learn discipline and emotional control rather than emotional self-expression. As Federici argues, the availability of a stable, well-disciplined labour force is an essential condition of production.[59] This emotional stability is therefore one of the main functions of emotional reproduction. Fortunati writes that 'the continual reproduction of the working class, which is essential for capital, depends on these relationships, so too does its productivity, its work discipline and adaptation to a whole complex of living conditions'.[60] Capacities for management of negative emotions, both one's own and those of others, are increasingly central in working-class jobs in the service economy. This requires a high level of self-control – the ability to keep smiling even while facing emotional abuse.

This regulation of feeling creates the need for a space outside of work where people do not need to perform the same emotional deference as they are compelled to at work. Emotional reproduction is not just oriented towards the suppression of bad feeling. It is also about creating an emotional sphere outside of waged work – a site supposedly free from work discipline. Emotional reproduction has a compensatory function. It is not only about creating emotional discipline but also about creating zones that are seemingly outside of emotional regulation, which can make up for the suppression of feeling in the workplace. The family and the community must provide some emotional satisfaction for those whose work conditions are the opposite of satisfactory. While women have been charged with a lot of waged and unwaged work, they often have to do some work of creating the home as an apparent site of non-work, of leisure and relaxation, obscuring their own labour in the domestic sphere.

Groups that face social marginalisation also have to engage in more compensatory types of emotional reproduction oriented towards healing the harms of oppression. The emotional costs of racism, homophobia, and transphobia can be severe, and marginalised people often seek to address these harms within their own communities. While this can create collectivities constituted against dominant forms of reproduction and ideology, it can also lead to increased emotional depletion and strain on those who are made responsible for healing the emotional harms caused by a hostile society. This is especially the case when emotional reproduction is individualised and possibilities for more collective responses to emotional harm are reduced.

In thinking about emotional reproduction, we should also consider the material sites where care takes place. Working-class sociality has historically not been confined to the privatised home to the same extent as bourgeois emotional reproduction. But forms of sociality that extend beyond the domestic space are constantly under threat. The spatial organisation of working-class emotional reproduction is vulnerable to destruction, as the public spaces that constitute an important precondition for many less privatised forms of sociality are increasingly rare. Stephanie Coontz, looking at the working-class organisation of space in the early twentieth century, notes that there was a lack of distinction between the intimate life of the family and the social life of the neighbourhood.[61] However, these spatial constructions of emotional life are difficult to sustain in the increasingly privatised landscape of contemporary capitalism. Gentrification poses a threat to those spaces that supported a wider set of social bonds in working-class communities. Domestic architecture has played a part in institutionalising the nuclear family as the most important form of sociality. The suburban one-family home, where the family is physically separated from other people, has become an aspirational sign of the good life. The emotional and social needs of people are codified in the built environment, creating boundaries for sociality. This institutionalisation of the nuclear family model often creates loneliness and a lack of emotional satisfaction for those who have been excluded from the family.

The reproduction of the working class is both influenced by and resistant to bourgeois values. The different needs that arise from the conditions of life of working-class and bourgeois people also create different demands on those performing this work. If the emotional reproduction of the middle and upper classes tends to involve the work of creating class aspiration, the reproduction of working-class life might entail more compensatory types of emotional labour. Emotional reproduction is class-specific, shifting according to various historical and social environments. In the past few decades, emotional services have become increasingly commodified, while also construed as the responsibility of individuals and families.

Commercialising Feeling

As neoliberal regimes have brought an increased commodification of reproduction, and more reproductive services can be bought from private companies, emotional labour has also become part of the services we buy. Some of the literature on emotional labour frames the political problem of emotional wellbeing in terms of its increasing commodification as part of the growing service economy. But the problems of emotional reproduction are not only associated with commodification. Emotional reproduction within the family is also exploitative and unfree. In both waged and unwaged forms of emotional labour, people often cannot meet their own needs without engaging in work under harmful, limiting, and exploitative conditions. The commercialisation of reproduction leads to a reconfiguration of emotional labour, but it is not always worse, or more capitalist, than doing it for free within the family or the community. Critiques of the commodification of reproductive labour, and emotional reproduction in particular, often become moralistic, and unwaged labour within the family is romanticised and seen as inherently anti-capitalist.

We need a more complex understanding of the role of emotional reproduction under capitalism. The privatisation of the home has come to create an internal outside of the capitalist economy, which has to appear untarnished by capitalist processes of valorisation. As Maya Gonzalez and Jeanne Neton argue, there must be an exterior to value in order for value to exist.[62] While the terms of this division between value and non-value are continually open to renegotiation through political struggle, the private sphere remains a constitutive outside of capitalist production – an outside which is essential to the functioning of capitalism while remaining seemingly external to it. Bourgeois distinctions between private and public mean that the family is often seen as non-political. Especially in writings on emotional labour, it is apparent that many on the left share the

bourgeois, sentimental vision of the family and emotional reproduction, a haven in a heartless world now renamed 'the potential for a kind of spontaneous and elementary communism'.[63]

Waged reproductive workers, such as carers and domestic
workers, are at the centre of much of the contemporary debate
on reproductive labour. Often migrant women of colour, their
labour is introduced as a solution to the crisis of social reproduction that has emerged both as a result of women's struggle
against unwaged labour and capital's increased use of women's
waged labour.[64] The current configuration of reproduction
has not abolished domestic work but rather shifted some of
it onto public or commodified service-provision or waged
domestic workers. Many of these jobs are low-paid and highly
exploitative. Care work often depends on creating emotional
bonds between the worker and the recipient of care, which
means that these bonds are more easily exploitable. In childcare, for instance, parents can use the bond between the carer
and the child to extract more labour than they are paying for.
While many mothers resist 'being replaced' by a nanny or
daycare worker as the child's primary caregiver, parents also
expect a high emotional standard from their replacement
caregivers, and are often happy to exploit the bond between
the caregiver and the child.[65] These forms of exploitation are
nothing new, as the bourgeois nuclear family has always relied
on the unseen labour of others. Simplified narratives of the
shift towards commodification often neglect this fact.

The commodification of care is related to not only the
arrangement of waged work and the family but also changing
constructions of need. While the working class as a whole has
struggled for a higher standard of living, members of this class
are seen as having varying needs. For instance, white workers
typically have a higher standard of living than black workers,
and can also expect a higher degree of emotional comfort and
care. The commodification of some emotional services might
be the result of increased emotional standards and more leisure

time. Higher standards of living often translate into greater access to emotional services for the wealthy. As Emma Dowling writes, services that cater to wealthy customers generally place greater weight on the delivery of emotional services.[66] Those at the top of social hierarchies can expect more attention to their individual emotional needs and a greater degree of emotional wellbeing. Commodification processes contribute to this tendency, as the rich are able to pay for the emotional services they need.

The growing service sector has led to more forms of emotional labour being carried out for a wage. As the capitalist labour market changes, the skills required of workers will also change. This might involve shifting standards for the mental and emotional constitution of individuals. Some workers need only minimally disciplined behaviour, whereas others need many years of intense subjectivation to various forms of emotional pressure. A changing labour market will also involve changing forms of emotional reproduction, as reproduction tends to be responsive to the demands of waged work.

The commodification of emotional labour hands over control of this work from individual men to capitalists, which might lead to more explicit forms of control and measurement. Despite the seemingly infinite character of emotional labour, Federici notes that capitalists have done their best to find ways to manage and measure this work.[67] Much of the literature on emotional labour explores how this control takes place. But in many cases, control is not only a result of the scripting and codification of emotional labour. Instead, its management involves cultivating a certain personality in the workers, thus integrating the work with the worker.[68] Hochschild notes how flight attendants are carefully screened before they are hired to ensure that they have the right character for interpersonal work.[69] In a different study of hiring panels for flight attendants, participants reported that they wanted to hire personalities that had a natural capacity for delivering emotional services – personalities which in most cases were feminine.[70] Companies come to rely on internalised forms of emotion management, which are seen as part of the worker's personality, as well as carefully codified external regulations. While measurability becomes central to the capitalist commodification and regulation of this work, it continues to draw on the supposedly natural personality of the worker, which in some sense exceeds that regulation and creates conditions for hyper-exploitation.

Measure and control have the effect of making emotional labour into specific and finite tasks to be completed by the worker. Commodification in some cases implies the loss of the infinite character of love. As emotional labour is scripted by company manuals, it becomes divided into discrete and measurable activities. When emotional labour is directed and controlled by employers, the social rules of emotion which are normally implicit become explicitly stated. Hochschild describes this as a form of unskilling of emotional labour, whereby agency over the work is increasingly removed from the worker.[71] However, Robin Leidner argues that the routinisation of emotional labour might help workers control service interactions.[72] The scripting of emotional labour may afford workers some control in relation to customers, though not in relation to managers.

The codification of emotional labour does not necessarily mean that workers are doing only what they are told, as workers in some situations might feel compelled to give more emotional care than they are explicitly asked to. This is particularly true across the public sector, including healthcare and education, which has faced significant cuts in recent decades, with resulting management calls for speed-ups and therefore less time for the labour-intensive work of creating good feeling. Workers might therefore feel compelled to do this work outside of their formal job description. As Dowling writes, when care is redefined as physical tasks, emotional aspects of care become unpaid.[73] In some types of care work, such as nursing, workers thus come to offer individualised emotional labour as a 'gift' to those they care for.[74] Nurses and carers may sit with a patient for a bit longer, to attend not only to their physical needs but to their need for social interaction and comfort. Emotional labour might not be formally integrated into the service itself, which is focused on the completion of physical tasks, yet management might rely on the empathy and sense of duty of its workers to provide emotional support for free. This allows for the hyper-exploitation of the caring capacities of already devalued groups of workers.[75]

The work of love involves tailoring emotional services to the specificity of the individual, thus continually reaffirming that very individuality in the process. The commercialisation of intimate services seems to imply the loss of this capacity, as services become increasingly standardised by management control. But capitalist production does not automatically lead to standardisation. Capitalist logics, when it comes to both the production of status and the production of services, rely on both standardising and individualising processes. High-end emotional services are often individually tailored as a part of their commodification. Certain forms of emotional labour and care services are thus limited to those who have the means to pay for them. For example, therapy and other forms of care that enhance mental wellbeing are difficult to access for those who cannot pay. The satisfaction of emotional needs is sometimes tied to access to commodities and services, and capitalism continually generates new needs that can only be satisfied through the market. Leisure activities, for instance, are highly commodified.

Critiques of the commercialisation of emotional services often implicitly suggest that the nuclear family is the proper site of emotional reproduction. According to these accounts, the family is under threat from the unfeeling logic of capitalism. Hochschild writes that 'part of the *content* of the spirit of capitalism is being *displaced* onto intimate life', suggesting that it was not present there before.[76] But the emotional life of the family has always been bound up with the reproduction of capitalism. And while commodified services cannot meet the needs of most people, the private sphere is also insufficient for meeting our needs. The nuclear family is not just one social form among others. Rather, it has been institutionalised as the exclusive site for catering to people's emotional needs. Unwaged forms of emotional reproduction are therefore often only accessible for those who are part of a nuclear family. Those excluded from the family often experience loneliness and a lack of emotional support. Other kinship forms have become less stigmatised, and the father-mother-child model has become more flexible, but the hegemonic status of the nuclear family still means that this form is promoted at the expense of other forms of sociality.[77] It is inscribed across legal, material, and ideological structures. Those who live outside the nuclear family, or are the primary caregivers within families, lack much of the emotional support that the family supposedly has been created to provide.

How we understand the distinction between private and public determines our political perspective on emotional reproduction. Those who view the domestic sphere as the proper place of emotional labour also tend to posit private and commercial forms of emotional reproduction as wholly distinct, valorising the supposedly more authentic private forms. But we can recognise the continuities of emotional labour across public and private spheres while at the same time emphasising that different logics of capitalist accumulation operate in these domains. Federici and Nicole Cox write that the ideology that opposes private and public supports the subjugation of women in the home, as it makes unwaged work appear as an act of love.[78] The division of private and public has very real effects, but mainly because it produces different forms of exploitation. The common understanding of the concept of work to mean only waged work serves to make unwaged work invisible and furthers its exploitation. The constitution of a private sphere, seemingly beyond labour law, also deepens the exploitation of waged domestic workers.[79] As domestic workers are presented as being 'part of the family', their work also assumes the character of private obligation, which facilitates increased exploitation.

The logic of capitalism is always present in the construction of the family and the community, and vice versa. This also means that the commodification of emotional labour and other forms of reproductive labour stems not only from the encroachment of capital logics upon private life but also from women's refusal of unwaged reproductive labour.[80] Camille Barbagallo argues that the use of commodified reproductive services might be seen as a passive and individualised form of resistance to the neoliberal logic which seeks to place responsibility for forms of care, previously provided by the welfare state, in the private household.[81] Arguing that emotional labour should be decommodified assumes the continued unwaged exploitation of women, at least in the absence of other forms of sociality that could provide less hierarchical and exploitative forms of emotional support.

It is not possible to commodify all reproductive labour. Because we tend to think of love as the opposite of money, there is a limit to the commercialisation of emotional reproduction. Some emotional labour is continually relegated to the private sphere, while other forms have moved into waged workplaces and the service economy. The public sphere and the commercial one are often constructed as devoid of feeling and ruled by rationality, whereas they are in fact suffused with emotion. Challenging some of the romanticised notions of the family as the proper sphere for feeling and care helps us understand how capitalism relies on emotional reproduction. Rather than being the opposite of the logic of capitalism, then, the family is in fact an integral part of this logic. This perspective is essential for beginning to resist capitalist logics of feeling.

2

The Political Economy of Love

There is so much work that goes into keeping us alive and healthy. Food needs to be prepared, houses cleaned, children looked after. We all need other people to care for us. Emotion cannot be understood in isolation from our other needs. We therefore have to situate emotional reproduction within the context of social reproduction more broadly. Otherwise, emotional labour comes to seem like a problem for a particular group of waged workers, and not something that happens across a range of sites and relationships in capitalist society. Through this broader understanding of emotional reproduction, we can view it not as something that emerged with the neoliberal service economy, but as an integral aspect of capitalist domination of our lives, needs, and desires.

The work that goes into meeting our needs has looked very different in various periods of history, as our needs are profoundly social and historical. While the need for food is a biological reality, how we satisfy our hunger looks very different in different epochs and among different classes within the same society. Moreover, different societies give rise to different types of needs. By needs, we should understand not only the things that we need to survive, but what we have come to expect as a decent standard of life. This could be something like access to public transport to get to work or being able to go out for a drink at the end of the week. All of our needs will have to be satisfied by specific forms of work, including our needs for social life and emotional comfort. Our needs, as we currently know them, are structured by capital's drive to accumulate value. The majority of people do not have access to the things they need unless they can find waged work.

Capital is more than just the organisation of factories or the ownership of the means of production. It is a set of social relations that structure life and work. The separation of workers from the resources they need to live should be understood as a relation of power, rather than just the ownership of things. In capitalism, value is created through labour, and power is expressed through the domination of labour. A commodity's value is determined by the length of time it would take the average worker to produce that good or service. Workers produce goods and services that are worth more than what the capitalist has paid to produce them. This is because workers are not paid for the labour itself, but instead something called labour power – their capacity to perform labour. This is what workers sell when they sign a contract with their employer.

The value of labour power is measured according to the value of commodities that the worker needs to survive – to pay for a historically specific minimum standard of basics such as food, housing, transport, and clothes. This means that capitalists can extract surplus value, which is the difference between the value that the worker has produced and what the capitalist pays the worker. Surplus value forms the basis of capitalist profit. Capitalist accumulation is founded on workers producing more value than they are paid for.

Capital has dispossessed most people of what they need to survive. It is not a system driven by meeting people's needs; instead, its only drive is to accumulate value. But a majority of workers need to be kept alive in order to maintain the extraction of value, because it is the labour of workers that creates value in the first place. A thing or service becomes a valuable commodity because it takes a certain number of hours for a worker to produce it. Individual capitalists will place the drive to make profit above the wellbeing of their workers. But if capitalist society overall functioned in this way, the working class would not be able to keep itself alive. This would in turn jeopardise the capitalists' use of human labour to create value. In capitalism, reproduction is generally subordinated to production and profit-making. But this primacy of production continually threatens the overall reproduction of capitalism as a system. There is a contradiction at the heart of the capitalist economy – workers are both individually disposable and collectively indispensable. This tension means that reproduction can become a central location of conflict and struggle, as its standards, resources, and labours are never simply given but are continually contested. The needs of capital, the state, and the workers themselves often come into contradiction. For example, it is in the interest of working-class people that sick pay and maternity pay are as generous and accessible as possible, but the interest of capital is usually to reduce all welfare benefits to the minimum level required for the working class to survive. Otherwise, the capitalists fear, it might become too easy for working class people to live without adhering to the discipline of wage labour.

In response to the bourgeois understanding of the private sphere as fully cut off from the public, and therefore non-political, it might be tempting to conclude that reproduction is fully capitalist, in the sense of responding to the demands of production. Capitalist production does dominate reproduction, but the two are also interdependent, as production could not exist without the work that goes into reproducing the labour force. Our needs are responsive to the demands of production, but can sometimes exceed them. The fact that reproduction has its own contradictions and antagonisms under capital means that it cannot be fully subordinated to the logic of production. Struggles on the site of reproduction can have an impact on the organisation of waged work, and have at times led the state to regulate the productive economy.

Certain types of labour are excluded from calculations of value, and such exclusions are themselves necessary for the production of value. Capitalist economies have to at least partly externalise the cost of reproduction. Instead of including unwaged reproductive labour in the value of labour power, capital posits reproduction as the individual responsibility of the worker. Unwaged reproductive work functions as a constitutive outside of capitalist economies – it is external to the formal wage relation, but capitalism could not sustain itself without it. A large proportion of reproductive labour has to remain unpaid for the capitalist economy to function, otherwise the value of labour power would simply be too high and capitalists would not be able to extract surplus value. For example, we typically buy food that is not fully prepared, and some additional unwaged work has to go into cooking the food so that it lives up to the standards we are used to. If all that work was paid, food would become incredibly expensive, like having takeaway every day. This would in turn drive up the value of labour power, and reduce the difference between the value of labour power and the total value produced by labour. If reproduction was valued like any other work, therefore, capitalism would no longer be profitable. This connection between reproductive labour and the value of labour power means that reproductive work is generally poorly paid and regarded as unskilled, if it is seen as work at all.

Reproduction is labour-intensive and mostly carried out at a relatively low level of technological development. The domestic technology that was introduced during the twentieth century did not significantly reduce the time spent performing reproductive labour, partly because the introduction of new machines coincided with increased standards for cleanliness and food preparation, as well as increased expectations of how much time should be spent on childcare.[1] As Silvia Federici puts it, 'The only true labor saving devices women have used in the '70s have been contraceptives.'[2] Some forms of reproductive labour depend on the continual presence of the worker, which means that it is difficult to make them more efficient. For example, childcare depends on someone being around all the time, attending to the needs of the child. While reproduction has been increasingly commodified over the past decades, it is difficult to fully integrate within the capitalist organisation of production, because to fully recognise it as work and to pay it accordingly would threaten capitalist accumulation. Moreover, the labour-intensive nature of reproduction often makes it difficult to turn it into a profitable service, and many companies in the care sector rely on state subsidies to make a profit.[3]

Unwaged reproductive labour is not accounted for in the value of labour power. The wage appears as a fair compensation for the hours spent doing waged work, not for the process of reproducing oneself or others as labour power. The employment contract itself conceals reproductive labour. The person with a primary responsibility for reproducing labour power is not constructed as the creator of that commodity but is alienated from it through a model of capitalist ownership of the self, which does not account for one's dependency on other people. Only the worker themself can enter a contract with an employer.

Not everyone has someone else to perform reproductive work for them – many workers do this for themselves as best they can. But everyone has at some point been cared for by someone else. The employment contract, through which labour power is sold as a commodity, excludes these social relations within which labour power is produced. The worker's capacities become naturalised as inherent in the worker, rather than acquired and historically specific. These capacities are seen no longer as social but as the private property of the worker. Emotional capacities are always social, but tend to be seen as expressions of the worker's authentic and pre-social personality.

Capitalism is structurally dependent on reproductive labour, both waged and unwaged. Because labour power is the central commodity of capitalist economies, the production of labour power is necessary work. As Federici writes, 'If we were not at home doing housework, none of their factories, mines, schools and hospitals could run, none of their profits could flow.'[4]

In contemporary capitalism, there has been an increased reliance on commodified reproductive services, yet these are also not always recognised as necessary for the functioning of the economic system more broadly. The commodification of reproduction might have made these activities more visible *as work*. When an activity becomes waged and performed for strangers, it is often difficult to keep pretending it is done purely out of love or as an expression of the personality of the worker. But this visibility has not always led to an acknowledgement of the dependency of value-producing labour on various forms of reproductive labour. Increased visibility does not necessarily change the material conditions of reproduction, which has been marginalised by the organisation of waged productive work. The commodification of reproductive services does not resolve the contradictory nature of reproduction under capitalism.

Today, many people rely on a combination of commodified and non-commodified reproductive labour. Commodification has been part of the restructuring of reproductive labour under the neoliberal regime, but much of the necessary work of reproducing labour power is still unwaged or provided by the state. Some of these tasks, especially the more physical forms of labour such as cooking and cleaning, can be outsourced to low-waged reproductive workers. But reproduction is more than the totality of discrete tasks. The patchwork of commodified and state-provided services has not fully replaced the labour traditionally done by women for their family members.

Reproductive work within the family often serves to create a more coherent form of care, which is better able to meet the specific needs of individuals. This type of care also addresses our emotional needs. Emotional bonds are central for ensuring the links between various types of reproductive work. In her 1975 pamphlet 'Wages against Housework', Federici writes:

> It is precisely this peculiar combination of physical, emotional and sexual services that are involved in the role women must perform for capital that creates the specific character of that servant which is the housewife, that makes her work so burdensome and at the same time so invisible.[5]

While the role of the housewife has more or less disappeared, most people still rely on their family members to meet at least some of their needs. The reproduction of people depends on some stability over time, even when the exact type of care they need changes. As members of the New York Wages for Housework Committee write, older women often take care of their grandchildren to allow their children to perform waged labour.[6] We continue to rely on family members to care for us and our own dependants, even when we are adults and seemingly more independent. Reproduction is a complex network of relations and dependencies, even in a neoliberal era which seemingly privileges individualism.

The Skills of Care

Because reproductive labour has to attend to a lot of different needs, it is a complex and skilled type of work. Being able to meet various needs requires a form of subjectivity that is attuned to the needs of others as well as the skills to perform reproductive tasks at a high standard. This work is not easily captured by the provision of commodified or state-provided reproductive services, because they are typically (though not exclusively) more standardised and impersonal. They therefore cannot perform the same role as the intimate work of care that takes place in people's homes and communities. As we saw in the last chapter, through the tailoring of care to suit the individual needs of the recipient, reproductive work helps people form a sense of being a unique and valued individual. This means that unwaged reproductive labour is often essential for fulfilling our emotional need for personal recognition. Unwaged reproductive work is infinitely complex, as it helps shape the difference between individuals through the satisfaction of individualised needs. Despite the complexity of care, it appears simple and unskilled. It is people's (and in particular women's) supposedly natural and spontaneous emotional and reproductive capacities that makes this work seem simple – in fact, it is not seen as work at all. This naturalisation of reproductive work operates despite or because of the fact that in capitalism, the subordination of reproduction to production continually threatens to disrupt the reproduction of labour power.

Under capitalism, workers become the carriers of labour power, a set of historically specific and produced skills and subjectivities that can be sold for a wage. According to Karl Marx, labour power is constituted by 'the aggregate of those mental and physical capabilities existing in the physical form, the living personality of a human being'.[7] Leopoldina Fortunati writes that these 'acquired and historically determined attributes ... are not homogeneous in all individuals'.[8] This is because our mental and physical capabilities are deeply social and are constituted differently according to our position within social hierarchies.

Skills and capacities are often presented in bourgeois ideology as natural and inherent in the worker. But in fact, we can begin to see how labour power consists of acquired capacities bound to the construction of gender and race. For example, within racial capitalism, black women have often been regarded as naturally suited for menial domestic labour such as cleaning and other 'dirty work'. Gendering and racialisation can be understood as a set of skilling and deskilling processes, where various skills are learnt from childhood. This challenges the framework of the capitalist construction of particular capacities as natural.

The demands of the labour market and the commodification of our capacity to work both shape and are shaped by historically specific arrangements of reproductive labour. The capitalist mode of reproduction forces us to reproduce *as labour power* – that is, as mere carriers of our capacity for particular forms of labour. Federici writes that understanding reproductive work as the production of labour power highlights 'the fact that in capitalist society reproductive work is not the free reproduction of ourselves or others according to our and their desires'. It also emphasises 'the tension, the potential separation, and it suggests a world of conflicts, resistances, contradictions that have political significance'.[9] Labour power is unique among commodities in that it is inseparable from the workers – people with needs, desires, and a capacity to struggle against the conditions of labour. It is the only commodity which has the capacity to resist its own conditions of production. But being reproduced as labour power also constrains those desires and capacities. The devaluation of workers takes place simultaneously with their constitution as value-creating labour power – we have to be worth less, and have fewer and cheaper needs and desires, in order to produce more value.

We are never reproduced fully for capital, nor for ourselves as people. Reproduction is both a site of preservation of the status quo and a potential space for the radical remaking of the world. This tension enables a feminist struggle in the sphere of reproduction, a struggle which has the potential to disrupt the functioning of capitalist society. As members of Wages for Housework argue, struggles on the site of reproduction subvert 'the image of social peace that has given capitalism the appearance of naturalness and viability'.[10]

But it is not easy to disentangle the different aspects of reproduction, and reproduction 'for ourselves' is not an uncomplicated matter. This is partly because we are currently forced to reproduce in ways that maintain social divisions and harm other people. The privatisation of reproduction means that one person's comfort and wellbeing often implies another person's depletion and unmet needs. The workers who can afford it may pay other workers starvation wages to look after their children or elderly relatives. These relations of exploitation are often drawn along lines of race and migration status. The working class is not a coherent unit with the same conditions of life. Some workers have a higher standard of life and more leisure time, while others live and work in degrading and harmful conditions. There is always a risk of romanticising the community or the domestic sphere, which appears as something totally distinct from capital and a space of freedom rather than exploitation. But hierarchies between workers stem not only from a stratified labour market but also from hierarchies within the sphere of reproduction.

The fact that we reproduce ourselves not only for capital but also for ourselves enables men to exploit the reproductive labour of women. To exploit the labour of other members of the class is also to reproduce for capital, since such exploitation reproduces the hierarchies of race and gender on which capital thrives. We are exploited when we are compelled to work for others, either by force or because we have to work to meet our own needs, but we receive less back than what we put into that work. Women tend to be exploited insofar as they cannot satisfy their own needs other than by labouring for other people. Often the only way women can have the economic security they need is through entering romantic relationships with men – relationships that tend to involve doing a lot of reproductive work. Men, on the other hand, often benefit from this labour because they tend to be the beneficiaries of women's caring work, and because they are largely freed from performing caring work for others. They are often excused from fully reciprocating women's care and from the work of caring for children, the elderly, and other dependants. Workers who have the option of exploiting the labour of others have an advantage over those who do not, since that gives them more time for their waged work and more leisure time to restore their capacity for labour.

Feminists have often argued that reproduction must be made visible as work. But the point is not to make reproductive work visible for visibility's own sake, or to morally valorise it. We need to be careful not to valorise or glorify reproductive work as we currently know it. Rather, feminist struggle strives to highlight capital's structural yet disavowed dependence on reproductive labour in order to subvert both this work and capital itself. It is by highlighting relations of power in our daily lives that we can struggle against them. In this way, we can multiply the sites of anti-capitalist struggle – expanding it from the workplace to the supposedly private domestic sphere. We strive to expand the ways we can reproduce ourselves for ourselves rather than for capital. In this, we must also challenge the relations of exploitation that take place between members of the working class. This means learning to care for each other not just as workers and family members, but as people with the capacity to resist capitalism. A central reason for struggling within the sphere of reproduction is to challenge hierarchies between workers in order to create a more unified working class, on the basis of the needs and demands of the most exploited within the class.

Permanent Reproductive Crisis

In post-war European and North American society, a combination of state services and unwaged domestic work constituted the main forms of reproductive labour. But today, a majority of women are also waged workers, which means that there is less time for unwaged domestic work. Austerity measures and cuts to healthcare and education mean that people generally have less access to state-provided services. Commodified reproductive services, provided by private companies, have been introduced to compensate for the fact that non-commodified reproductive labour is less available. But the labour-intensive and often less profitable nature of reproductive work means that it has not been fully commodified, and some previously waged reproductive labour has in fact been pushed back into the sphere of unwaged work.[11] Many working-class people cannot afford commodified reproductive services but continue to rely on poorly resourced state-provided services and unwaged reproductive labour. Today, some reproductive labour happens through public–private partnerships, where the state funds private companies to provide reproductive services.

This lack of resources for reproductive labour has led to a diagnosed 'crisis of care' or 'crisis of social reproduction'. In one account, the crisis emerged because of the combined decline of the welfare state and the family model in which men were breadwinners and women housewives. But this more recent crisis is only the open manifestation of the underlying contradiction of capitalist reproduction, which has always been a feature of capitalism. Federici calls this a permanent reproductive crisis.[12] Some accounts of the crisis of care tend to obscure the fact that some groups have always experienced reproductive crises, but that these crises are not expressed evenly. Instead, it has dramatically different effects on different groups. The idea that a crisis of care has emerged with neoliberalism conceals how the post-war, supposedly non-crisis organisation of reproduction never included everyone, even within North American and European countries. Rather, this model of reproduction imposed differentiated and hierarchical reproductive standards. Some people's needs were met by the state and the breadwinner/housewife family model, while other people's needs were neglected. Reproduction under capitalism is always stratified along lines of class, race, and migration status. This corresponds to a stratification of wages, as those who have been forced to reproduce at a lower standard are also paid less for their labour power – their capacity to labour is worth less but produces more surplus value.

Those who are excluded from the labour market have to rely on the state, family members, community services, or criminalised activities to survive. These forms of reproduction are often stigmatised, for example through the images of 'welfare queens' and 'benefit cheats' – racialised stereotypes that also carry associations of stigmatised sexual behaviour and bad reproduction. Those who survive outside of the normative pattern of wage labour and family are seen as reproducing deviant forms of life.

Various kinds of reproductive work are also valued differently, depending on the nature of that labour, who is performing it, and for whom it is performed. Evelyn Nakano Glenn points to the racialised differentiation of reproductive work, in which emotional and customer-oriented labour has been more highly valued than the 'dirty', manual, and backroom forms that have often been reserved for women of colour and migrants.[13] The reproduction and survival of stigmatised groups is seen as less important in capitalist societies. While white, middle-class, and bourgeois people can expect longer, healthier lives, others are, as Ruth Wilson Gilmore puts it, made vulnerable to premature death.[14] The different valuation of various forms of reproduction therefore reflects and recreates deep splits and hierarchies within the working class.

Neoliberal capitalism is seemingly hostile to reproduction. Neoliberal states have typically cut state provision of reproductive services, and increased automation within the contemporary economy seemingly makes capitalism less dependent on human labour. This makes it appear that the state and capital are no longer interested in the reproduction of human life. But contemporary capitalism is as dependent on reproductive work as previous forms of accumulation, and as dependent on living

labour. Only human labour can produce new value, and workers cannot be fully replaced by machines. Even though core
capitalist economies are increasingly producing surplus populations – people who are temporarily or permanently excluded
from wage labour – the exclusion of these groups does not
mean that their existence is superfluous to the functioning of
the capitalist economy.

People belonging to surplus populations might be more aware
of the permanent nature of the reproductive crisis, where their
lives and deaths do not seem to matter much to capital or the
state. But capital relies on the continued existence of vulnerable
surplus populations. In her study of temporary women workers
in China and Mexico, Melissa Wright shows how entire groups
of people are produced as temporary and disposable resources
in terms that also make individual workers vulnerable to violence
and death.[15] These groups can be employed and laid off as
needed in the short-term expansion and contraction of the
labour market, and they are produced as cheap labour power
whose reproduction costs capital next to nothing. The state has
often had a role in controlling the reproduction of these groups,
simultaneously trying to reduce the cost of their reproduction
through limiting access to welfare and ensuring that they are still
reliant on capitalist regimes of work by criminalising and stig-
matising non-wage-based forms of life. While they are partially
excluded from waged labour, the state tries to prevent these
groups from inventing ways of surviving fully outside of capitalist circuits of production and reproduction.

Organisations led by women of colour have long struggled
against the stratification of reproduction, for example through
broadening the question of reproductive rights to include not
only access to abortion but also the struggle against forced
sterilisations. Wilmette Brown, a co-founder of Black Women
for Wages for Housework, writes that in the twentieth-century
United States, sterilisation was often a condition for receiving
a welfare check. She points to the long history of racial capital

when she writes that the 'population of black people has always been a burning issue for international capital: . . . it has never ceased to concern itself with the size, age, sex, availability, manageability, and when need be, extinction, of the black population as a labour force'.[16]

The purpose of capitalist reproduction, then, is to ensure not only the physical survival of the workers but also a disciplined workforce. It is not only the number of workers that is at stake but the availability and manageability of the labour force, as well as the discipline of reproductive workers. Capitalist states attempt to promote a specific type of reproduction – one that creates a stable, disciplined labour force where people have an affective investment in work and in preserving the current organisation of society, even when they are partially excluded from it. Only certain forms of reproduction are encouraged by state policies. The state disciplines supposedly bad reproductive subjects through welfare policies, lack of access to reproductive services, and incarceration. The state has had a central role in organising reproductive labour, which becomes especially clear in situations of heightened reproductive crisis, or as a manager for those who have been less willing to reproduce in a normative manner. Members of Wages Due Lesbians and Black Women for Wages for Housework struggled against the state's intervention into reproduction – forced sterilisations of black women and loss of custody rights for lesbians and other 'bad mothers'.[17] Because the sphere of reproduction is characterised by contradiction and tension, the state intervenes to maintain normative reproductive standards. This has led the state to be invested in creating normative family values which also serve to discipline those who resist the current reproductive order.

The state promotes what it deems to be good reproduction through welfare policies and normative family values. State policies are not just repressive but actively organise unwaged and waged reproductive labour. Mariarosa Dalla Costa writes:

In the era of mass production – not only in the material sense but its reproduction on the psychic level, including its discipline and socialization – in which the correlate production of a new labour power required a specific relationship between the family and the labor market, the state needed to both regulate the labor market and strengthen the family.[18]

The family, she concludes, was at the centre of the New Deal in the US and post-war welfare states more broadly, setting the standard for the type of reproductive labour that could produce a disciplined and relatively healthy population.[19] The welfare state, while seemingly replacing some of the labour of the family, actually operated in continuity with it, often intervening in the so-called private sphere. And while neoliberal regimes seem less reliant on traditional family forms, Melinda Cooper has shown that neoliberalism is based on normative family values, and operates on an often unspoken assumption of family support of the individual.[20] The family is an ideological and material supplement of the free individual assumed by neoliberalism. Our current political regime requires the continual management of reproductive labour and preserves some version of the family as a unit of reproduction and economic support. Inheriting assets such as a family home has become increasingly important for the economic stability of the middle class as waged work has become more precarious.

In times of open reproductive crisis, when the working class struggles to reproduce itself because of the harms created by waged work and poor living conditions, the state might intervene in the productive sphere. Fortunati shows how the modern, capitalist state was shaped by the open reproductive crisis caused by capitalist industrialisation in the nineteenth century, when workers, including children, were drawn into factory work to an extent that threatened the generational replacement of the working class. She cites Marx's comments on the 'unnatural estrangement' between mothers and infants that occurred in this phase of capitalist accumulation, which led to high rates of neglect and infanticide.[21] Working-class people died very young, both because of the crushing conditions of factory work and because of dire housing conditions and lack of access to healthcare. While individual capitalists are not particularly interested in the wellbeing of the working class, large-scale reproductive crises can become disruptive to the economy. In order to stave off this crisis, in which mothers lost their supposedly natural maternal instinct and young adults died or lost their ability to work, the state had to intervene in the productive sphere of waged work as well as the sphere of reproduction. It created limitations on the working day to ensure that the working class had the time and means to reproduce itself.[22] The total subordination of reproduction to the short-term interest of production – the extraction of value through the extension of the working day – was found to undermine the long-term stability of capitalist accumulation. The state, seeking to ensure such stability, was forced to intervene and regulate the length of the working day as well as general working conditions. Bourgeois philanthropy and working-class struggle in time created more stable conditions of reproduction, increasing the availability of reproductive resources such as decent housing, healthcare, and education. After the world wars, in a time of greater prosperity, the welfare state was created to 'solve' the crisis in reproduction, at least for some people. This phase of capitalism, however, was an exception, and the working class has always lived in a state of reproductive crisis.

Naturalisation and Privatisation

Capitalist society depends on the labour of reproduction, both waged and unwaged. To obscure the contradictory nature of reproduction under capitalism, reproductive labour is simultaneously glorified and made invisible, valorised, and devalued.

Bourgeois ideology celebrates a particular form of reproduction, both through the image of the self-sacrificing wife and mother and through the story that in order to have a good life, we must desire romance, a family, and a private family home. Emotional reproduction is intimately tied to the ideological notion that capitalist reproduction is overall good and desirable, as we come to associate good feelings with particular forms and relationships of reproduction. This valorisation of reproductive labour can reinforce the split between productive and reproductive work. This was most clearly the case in the Victorian valorisation of white women's care for their families – the ideological figure of 'the angel in the house', constructed as the opposite of the world of productive work and driven by love and altruism rather than individualism and profit. This glorification of the white bourgeois wife and mother obscured the contributions of domestic servants and other working-class women.[23] This type of valorisation does not translate into women's autonomy over their labour, nor does it challenge the conditions under which they work. Instead, it serves to increase women's attachment to reproductive labour as the source of the good life.

According to bourgeois ideology, the community and the family are part of private life, separate from the logic of the market. Bourgeois ideology both reflects and conceals the material organisation of capitalist reproduction. It has obscured how we reproduce ourselves as labour power – as workers selling our capacity to work to capitalists. The ideological split of private and public has real consequences for how people live their lives, and also serves to shore up the separation between production and reproduction. There is no strict spatial boundary between the private and the public, but these terms do name a certain experience of capitalist life. For example, there is an assumption that care belongs in the private sphere, and many people experience care at home as preferable to institutional forms of care. The work of reproduction takes place across multiple sites, but the private domestic sphere is still seen as the proper place for reproduction.

While the state and capital have always sought to regulate the reproduction of the working class, this sphere of life has often appeared as an entirely private matter. Reproduction has come to appear as non-political in a way that conceals its contradictions and antagonisms. This privatisation obscures the historically specific character of reproduction under capitalism, making current reproductive forms seem natural and desirable. The reproductive arrangement of the nuclear family seems like a personal choice and yet something that everyone wants. Within the sphere of reproduction, the capitalist primacy of production is inverted, and reproductive labour seems primary and natural. Fortunati writes that the limitation of the working day in the sphere of production coincided with the extension of the working day in the sphere of reproduction.[24] The reproductive crisis in the nineteenth century, when the working class was struggling to reproduce itself, in time led to improved conditions of reproduction for many sections of the population. This happened both through higher standards of housing and reproductive services and through an increase in the time that working-class women were expected to devote to taking care of their families. The new mode of capitalist accumulation that emerged towards the end of the nineteenth century, based on the intensification of labour rather than long working days, also required a more disciplined working class. Women had to train their children to become good and disciplined wage workers with an emotional attachment to the ideals of work and family. The reward for this increased discipline at the waged workplace was a supposedly more emotionally satisfying home life as well as increased access to consumer goods and commodified leisure activities.

This involved promoting ideologies of heterosexual romance and family as the ultimate goal of life. Heterosexual marriage has become synonymous with the good life, and everyone seemingly desires the normative reproductive arrangements of the nuclear family. Heterosexuality is the naturalisation of unwaged labour – through heterosexuality, the gendered division of labour becomes natural, desirable, and good. Romance ideology made emotional labour appear as a reward rather than work.

As Fortunati writes, the figure of the housewife functions as the inversion of the general logic of capital which subordinates reproduction to production.[25] She cannot appear as labour power on the waged labour market without simultaneously appearing to capital as a natural source of unwaged reproductive labour, and therefore as a person with responsibilities outside of waged work. The unwaged reproductive sphere continues to mark women as reproductive workers even as they enter the sphere of waged labour. Women's reproductive capacities are perceived as primary even for those who are neither mothers nor housewives. This primacy of reproduction makes women workers appear as ideal part-time waged workers, as they are assumed to have caring commitments. Lack of access to full-time work in turn increases women's economic precarity, which often means they have to rely on a man's wage to have a decent standard of life.

A disciplined workforce is shaped through discourses of individualisation and choice within the sphere of reproduction. The terminology of 'choice' of part-time work appears central for maintaining women's continued responsibility for reproduction. In this discourse, mothers who are waged workers simply 'choose' to earn less and spend more time taking care of their children. The discourse of individual choice points to the continuing relegation of reproductive labour to the private sphere and personal responsibility. Even in the current organisation of reproduction, when much of this work takes place outside of the home, it is still common sense that reproduction is essentially a private matter. But this does not lead to more freedom in the sphere of reproduction, since the available choices are so limited. Especially for those responsible for the reproduction of others, there is little material support for choices other than the most normative. For instance, there are very few options in terms of affordable childcare, and many people do not have personal relationships that could support childcare arrangements outside of the nuclear family.

Reproductive labour is privatised and appears non-political, despite constant state intervention. As Fortunati writes, the family appears to be 'the least capitalist relations that exist'.[26] This creation of an 'outside' of capitalist relations is an essential aspect of unwaged emotional reproduction, which appears natural and desirable in contrast with the regulation of waged work. As we saw in the last chapter, this privatisation has an important function within emotional reproduction – to individualise the recipient of reproductive labour. All privatised, unwaged care comes to appear as an investment in their person, strengthening their sense of personal value as well as satisfying some of their needs. Acts of physical labour can thus contribute to emotional reproduction because they give the recipient a sense of being cared for and therefore valued as a person. This care takes the person as an individual, especially if the acts of care are tailored to their supposedly unique and individual needs. This counteracts the de-individualising that many people experience at their waged workplaces, where they are fundamentally replaceable. Reproductive labour therefore appears to be outside the logic of capitalist markets, and provides people with a sense of individuality which compensates for their dehumanisation as labour power.

This individualisation is tied to ideologies of love and sexuality. Sex is supposedly the most private activity, which, according to bourgeois notions of propriety, is reserved for the bedroom. It is personal, natural, and supposedly stemming only from individual attraction – our sexual desires are

48

frequently portrayed as pre-social. As Federici points out, it is presented as the opposite of work and a free expression of individuality and pleasure.[27] Sex work and queer sexualities challenge this privatisation, as they have long been excluded from the domestic sphere and seen as disturbingly public and improper. Queer sex is less privatised due to the historical exclusion of queer people from the domestic sphere of the nuclear family. The incorporation of homosexuality within the nuclear family has changed this, as same-sex sexual practices have become increasingly privatised and seen as a personal lifestyle choice. The decriminalisation of sodomy in the US, which took place through the 2003 Supreme Court case *Lawrence v. Texas*, stipulated that gay sex should be legalised because of the protection of sexual privacy in the home.[28] Like queer sex, sex work has often been marked as a moral issue, partly because it mostly takes place outside of domestic settings, and partly because it challenges the understanding of sexuality as a private matter and the opposite of work. The private sphere is not just a domestic setting but the space for heteronormative, unpaid sex.

Some sexual practices can therefore be understood as a form of resistance to the privatisation of reproduction. Sexual practices can be mobilised as a form of reproduction for ourselves as politicised subjects. Sexuality is bound up with the practices of reproductive work (particularly for women in heterosexual relationships), but it can also create a space of subversive sociality. Especially for those whose sexual practices and identities are less closely tied to the intimate sphere of domestic heteronormativity, sexuality can become a way of reproducing differently. Queer sex can be understood as a form of refusal to reproduce within the bounds of capitalist reproduction. But this is only possible if we consider queer sex not merely as a personal choice or an individualised form of resistance, but as part of a wider struggle against the current arrangement of our intimate lives.

Reproductive Antagonisms

Heterosexuality is the naturalisation of reproductive labour, and reproductive work entails the naturalisation of capitalism. Feminists must challenge these forms of naturalisation. As members of the English Wages for Housework collective write, 'The routines of capitalist life have always given capital the appearance of naturalness (as if life couldn't be any other way) and the appearance of viability (as if nothing else could work as well).' They add that 'halting service work undermines this appearance of social peace'.[29] The work of Marxist feminist theory and organising, then, is to heighten antagonisms within the reproductive sphere, so that gendered work no longer appears as a natural fact.

Naming supposedly natural gendered capacities as work is one strategy for their denaturalisation. This is a form of separation and disentanglement – a way of saying that we could be more than our acquired capacities for labour. It paves the way for refusing to carry out reproductive labour, because that no longer seems like our natural destiny. It is a way of highlighting our dual existence as labour power and something more than labour power. In Kathi Weeks's terms, this naming constitutes a feminist subjectivity simultaneously created by and against the social relations of work.[30] As she puts it, struggles within the sphere of reproduction depend on our ability to create a distance between what we have been made into and what we could become.[31] Denaturalisation opens up possibilities for struggle, as it shows that the world could be completely different.

There are many sites of possible struggle within the varied field of reproduction. Fighting for the right to abortion, for example, has been a way of challenging the imperative to reproduce for capitalism. But some (mainly racialised and disabled) people are marked as undesirable reproductive subjects within racial-capitalist reproductive norms. Brown argues that for those who are typically excluded from normative forms of reproduction, having children might be a way of affirming the value of reproducing against the state and capital.[32] Raising those children against the demand for a disciplined labour force might also be a way of resisting capital accumulation.[33] By raising children who are not trained to love and respect their boss, we can increase the possibilities of workplace resistance.

Feminist struggles against capitalist reproduction emphasise the possibility of struggle from different points within the capitalist circuit and the potential power of refusal that belongs not only to workers in key sectors of industry but to all those who participate in capitalist economies in some capacity. This includes students, the unemployed, unwaged peasants, and housewives.[34] It also includes those seemingly 'unorganisable' members of the class who have an antagonistic relation to the state, such as people who are criminalised in various ways. Reproductive struggles could expand to include those who have traditionally been dismissed as belonging to the lumpen-proletariat – those who survive outside of the formal and legal economy. Struggles of recipients of care create a potential for solidarity between reproductive workers and those they care for – including children, the elderly, and the mentally ill. From the perspective of reproduction, we can understand capitalism as a broader system which includes informal economies and unwaged workers, and therefore many possible points of struggle.

The naming of reproduction as work opens up the possibility of refusing that work. But refusing reproductive labour can be difficult. The dual nature of reproduction – as reproduction of both labour power for capitalism and people for themselves – means that it is difficult to disrupt the reproduction of labour power without also harming people. Moreover, many types of struggles on the site of reproduction can become part of the expanded accumulation of capital. The paradigmatic case here is perhaps the nineteenth-century struggle for a shorter working day, which was at least partly based on a concern for reproduction, but which led to the intensification of work.[35] As the working day was shortened in the factory, workers were expected to speed up the pace of production to do an equal amount of work in a shorter period of time. Simultaneously, the length of the unwaged working day of housewives was extended through ever-increasing expectations of domestic standards and familial love. A more contemporary example is the use of low-waged migrant labour to 'solve' the current reproductive crisis, caused in part by white middle-class women's refusal of full-time reproductive labour.[36] This has led to more exploitative working conditions and precarity for migrants and the expansion of commodified, for-profit forms of care.

Struggles against unwaged reproduction thus risk harming those who are recipients of care, or risk increasing the exploitation of other reproductive workers while not threatening capital or the state. We need reproductive struggles that can address the concerns of reproductive work without displacing the potential harm of such struggles onto more marginalised groups, either recipients or workers. The working class can only be unified on the terms of those most marginalised by the current organisation of capitalism.[37] Feminist struggle over reproduction must do more than just reshuffle the responsibility for reproductive labour.

Through unwaged work, expensive reproductive resources, and 'individual responsibility', capital has externalised much of the cost of reproducing the labour force. Capital accumulation depends not only on waged work but also on the circulation and consumption of commodities, as well as the availability of labour power. Rather than just focusing on the disruption at the point of production of value, struggles over reproduction bring into view the full circuit of capitalist production. Interventions in reproduction and consumption can take various forms, including rent strikes, strategic withdrawals of unwaged labour, 'proletarian shopping' (collective and organised shoplifting), and the reappropriation of reproductive resources and services. These struggles can involve decommodifying reproductive resources, such as housing and healthcare. This can increase the cost of reproduction for capital and the state, and refuse individual responsibility for reproduction.

A way of struggling against the capitalist organisation of society is to create new social needs, such as free housing or childcare services, which continually increase the cost of reproducing the working class for capital and the state. For example, we can demand access to housing which facilitates and minimises domestic labour rather than making it more difficult and privatised. The point is not just to improve domestic working conditions but rather to undo the material and ideological lines between the domestic and the public, the reproductive and the productive, as these divisions currently serve to individualise responsibility and enable exploitation. Such undoing challenges the organisation of the totality of the capitalist circuit. Capital would not be able to fully internalise the cost of reproductive labour without becoming unprofitable. For the Wages for Housework activists, the aim is 'to be priceless, to price ourselves out of the market, for housework and factory work and office work to become "uneconomic"'.[38]

A radical perspective on reproduction means the refusal to internalise the cost and effort of reproducing the working class. It is a refusal of the notion that some members of the class must necessarily be exploited by others in order for people to survive and have decent lives. The demands for more money, more free time, and better reproductive services are also a demand for an end to the inadequate remuneration of all the work that people perform, and an end for the wage relation based on the invisibility and devaluation of reproductive labour. In organising communal reproductive resources, this could also expand our social worlds, which are currently often restricted to various labour relationships within waged and unwaged spheres. The current organisation of reproductive work tends to construct love as the reward for labour, yet love itself is part of the reproductive labour that people do for each other. Reproductive labourers try to produce the good life for other people in order to compensate for the damaged life of capitalist labour. We must demand more than this meagre reward. We do this by expanding the needs of the working class, creating collective forms of reproduction, and increasing the cost of reproduction for the capitalists. As Wages for Housework members put it: 'So far we have done it for love, not money. But the cost of loving is going up.'[39]

3
Gendering Work

Feelings are not non-political or private. They have deeply gendered connotations, and people are made to perform gender-appropriate feelings. The social rules for expressing emotion are different for men and women. But gender is not only about expressing or not expressing certain genuine, pre-social feelings – it also creates a sense of gendered interiority, which feels masculine or feminine because it has the capacity for particular emotions. Gendered feeling becomes a sign of our authentic selves. Shiloh Whitney writes that 'the affective laborer's deep acting achieves the effect of expressing an interiority that seems to precede the performance, but in fact is cultivated by it'.[1] Emotional labour contributes to the production of gendered interiority through the bodily performance of emotion.

The reproduction of society calls for a particular set of feelings seen as socially appropriate. Different feelings are the right ones in different social circumstances. For people to feel well, someone needs to create good feelings. These feelings of niceness are a core function of the bourgeois family. There can be a lot of work involved in creating a spirit of niceness at family dinners and holidays, where conflict needs to be held at bay. It is also a key feminine task – smoothing over conflict, soothing hurt feelings, creating a spirit of relaxation and wellbeing. Women are called to perform these tasks in their families, at work, and among friends and acquaintances. Niceness is a bourgeois family value which women are compelled to create through both domestic and emotional labour. In this way, the gendering of feeling reproduces a split subjectivity where women are tasked with creating relationality and emotional wellbeing, while men have licence to act as solitary individuals, affirming their own importance and worth over others.

This lens of emotional reproduction allows us to see how gender is intimately connected to work. The work that we do becomes part of how we experience ourselves as subjects. Our self-understanding of what types of work we can do, what skills we have, is closely linked to how we perceive ourselves as gendered subjects. Moreover, the process of becoming a properly gendered subject can itself be understood as a form of work – the labour we do on ourselves to manage our relation to gendered norms. Sometimes we work to live up to such norms, and sometimes we work to distance ourselves from them. The labour of becoming a gendered subject is never complete. Gender consists of ideal forms to which people are compelled to aspire, with varying degrees of success, not as forms that can be fully inhabited by any individual. While these forms are ideological, they are also both the results and the preconditions of gendered forms of labour. Gender ideals are often multiple and contradictory. It is impossible to fully adhere to idealised gender norms. These norms are a way of extracting a certain amount of labour, despite or because of the fact that fully living up to hegemonic gender ideals is an impossible goal. Women tend to be perceived, and perceive themselves, as more caring than men. Their very personalities therefore become conflated with a specific type of work: emotional reproduction.

Femininity as Work Function

Gender can be understood as the capacity for a certain type of labour. Femininity is not a naturally existing personality but a skill learnt from infancy. As Silvia Federici puts it, femininity is a work function.[2] This capacity, however, is deeply naturalised, as modern understandings of gendered difference have anchored hierarchies of gender in bodily types. The naturalisation of difference has led to an understanding of gender as inevitable biological destiny.[3] This serves to hide women's work *as work*, and instead conflates this labour with women's bodies and personalities. The construction of work as conscious activity has also obscured the fact that femininity is a work function, as feminine gender has become equated with bodily and emotional states, which are in turn constructed as passive. Gender, like emotion, is neither a passive state nor necessarily a fully conscious activity. But this does not mean that it is not work.

Women are active participants in gendered relations and not mere victims of patriarchy. Most people are made to work under conditions not of their own choosing, thus participating in the very relations that subordinate them. While gendered relations are exploitative for most women, they can also produce rewards for those who do gender well, in particular for white, bourgeois, heterosexual women who are able to perform femininity more or less according to normative stand-ards. Failure or refusal to live up to these norms can lead to violent punishment. Wilmette Brown explores how gendered ideals are co-constitutive with whiteness: 'White women are the legitimate objects of beauty, of love, of femininity. Black women are not.'[4] While the modern, capitalist construction of femininity is based on an idealised notion of white, hetero-sexual, and bourgeois women, it functions as a disciplinary tool cutting across race and class.

Gender is usually understood as expressive of a pre-existing authentic self rather than as a form of labour that needs to be constantly repeated. Federici writes that housework 'has been transformed into a natural attribute of our female physique and personality, an internal need, an aspiration, supposedly coming from the depth of our female character'.[5] A particular type of labour is thus seen as something coming from within the subject itself rather than an external imposition. Thinking of gender as a form of labouring subjectivity helps us understand how gender is both imposed on us and something we actively participate in. Kathi Weeks argues that an understanding of gender based on labour can help us move beyond both voluntarism and determinism, as the concept of labour invokes both constraints and continual, creative remaking. She understands the labour of gender as constitutive of an experience of relative coherence of the subject.[6] Gender emerges as an effect of labouring practices as well as a precondition for that labour, pointing to the constructedness yet relative stability of gendered subjectivity.

Not only have feminised subjects been made responsible for reproductive labour, but they also tend to have a primary responsibility for reproducing gender as such. This involves the work of affirming and enhancing other people's gender presentation. In heterosexual relationships in particular, women are tasked with the role of affirming their partner as a 'real man'.

Men also perform gendered labour, but of a different type. Within the domestic sphere, men tend to specialise in work that involves heavy lifting or technical skill, such as fixing things that are broken.[7] The work of masculinity tends to affirm the independence and competence of the subject, rather than its subordination to the needs of others. Men are thus excused from performing much of the work of caring for others, and can generally do less emotional work. There is a tendency to distribute the burden of reproductive labour onto feminised subjects and the rewards of such labour onto men. Men can reap the benefits of the reproductive labour of others. This is a form of exploitation. The exploitation of reproductive work operates through assumptions of heterosexual gendered complementarity, in which difference is constructed around the need for one's 'other half'. Women are the primary labouring subject in these relationships. Gendered capitalism functions through a series of ideological inversions, so that the exploiting subjects come to appear as active, independent, and universal, while the labouring subjects come to appear as dependent, passive, and particular. Through this notion of heterosexual complementarity, women come to appear as passive objects, as the opposite of active masculinity.

Gender is an inherently exploitative relation – women as a group are exploited by men as a group. Not all women are exploited nor are they all exploited to the same extent. Not all men benefit from the exploitation of women in comparable ways. But all feminised subjects are affected by the exploitation of a majority of women. As Diemut Elisabet Bubeck suggests, all women are vulnerable to gender-based exploitation, even if they as individuals are not exploited.[8] Heterosexual arrangements are exploitative in ways that benefit capital but also benefit men. It is crucial for the existence of this particular exploitative relation that it appears to be outside of capitalist monetary relations, and that it therefore appears as a natural and private bond of love.

Domestic Violence as Workplace Injury

While capitalism is the dominant mode of production within which all other forms of exploitation are situated, the wage relation between capitalist and worker is not the only relation based on the extraction of labour. Other forms of exploitation, such as the extraction of use values or surplus labour, are historically more common than exploitation based on surplus value.[9] While the extraction of surplus value is currently the dominant form of exploitation, other forms of exploitation did not disappear with the rise of capitalism. In fact, they are constitutive parts of the capitalist economy. We can see this in the organisation of the so-called informal economy, where labour is not organised by contractual wage relations but is nonetheless often integrated in capitalist production. Another example is when white, bourgeois, middle-class women transfer some of their domestic duties onto more marginalised workers. This is a form of exploitation based on surplus labour, constituted mainly along lines of race, migration status, and class. The compounded vulnerabilities of race, gender, and class leave working-class women of colour particularly likely to be exploited in the most strenuous and least valued types of reproductive labour. It is a way in which, as Dorothy Roberts suggests, some women's greater equality with men can lead to increased hierarchy and exploitation among women.[10]

The fact that the gendered exploitation of reproductive labour is not primarily or exclusively organised in terms of surplus value does not mean that gender-based exploitation should be understood as external to capitalism. The rise of capitalism created the conditions for the exploitation of reproductive labour as we know it. Capitalist extraction of surplus value depends on spheres of non-value. Gender-based exploitation is therefore not outside of capitalism, but neither does it necessarily operate according to the same logic that structures capitalist production. This does not mean that patriarchy is an independent system, nor is it pre-capitalist in its form. In order to counter the tendency to present patriarchy as transhistorical, we must be aware of both continuities and differences of gender relations in the transition to capitalism.

Gendered exploitation as we know it emerged through the violent social changes of early capitalism, and gendered forms of violence remain central to maintaining gendered forms of labour. Violence is inherent in exploitation. Sexual and domestic violence are not themselves the cause of gendered domination but effects of the need to control women's labour. Men's domination thus cannot be located in a masculine propensity for sadism. Gendered violence happens not for its own sake but for ensuring the continued reproduction of the world as we know it. Giovanna Franca Dalla Costa writes that violence cannot be understood separately from heterosexual constructions of love. Violence is thus not 'deviant' with regards to 'normal' heterosexual relationships. Even in heterosexual relationships that are not violent, violence figures as an unspoken possibility. Within romantic and familial relationships, violence is not love's opposite. Dalla Costa contends that violence is authorised by love because the marriage contract appears as a contract of love rather than labour, and thus love is what is 'owed' in the relation between spouses. Men have the right to use force to ensure that such emotional debts are paid.[11] As violence takes on the appearance of love, it becomes a tool for disciplining women's emotional labour. As Federici puts it, men can 'supervise our sexual work, to ensure that we would provide sexual services according to the established, socially sanctioned productivity norms'.[12] They can thus lay claim to women's bodies, energy, and time. The threat of gendered violence also acts to keep women in the domestic sphere, as sexual violence is often seen as the natural result of women's entrance into the public sphere.[13] Despite the fact that most violence against women happens within intimate relationships, dominant ideology portrays it as a result of women staying out too late at night or being in dangerous public places.

When women fail to enjoy or start resisting gendered work, they are met with various kinds of violence, both physical and emotional. One form of violence is the pathologisation of women's resistance to emotional labour. Federici writes that women are called insane when they resist housework, and 'going crazy' has historically been one of the only ways for women to get out of their responsibility for reproductive work.[14] Those who fail to perform and enjoy the naturalised labour of femininity, then, are likely to be pathologised, even criminalised. This is particularly the case for those who do not perform gendered labour within normative nuclear families. Brown notes that the ideal of the white bourgeois family functions as a disciplinary norm against which black families, and black women in particular, are pathologised.[15] This in turn justifies intense state surveillance of those women deemed deviant, as well as state intervention, such as the loss of custody of one's children, forced sterilisation, or the loss of benefits, if one does not do reproductive labour the right way.

Queer women are also subjected to punishments for their refusal of heterosexualised norms of femininity – forms of violence and exclusion that serve to warn other women not to become lesbians.[16] Heterosexuality can be understood as a form of discipline, or a work ethic.[17] It is from this work, and the approval that comes from it, that women learn to derive their sense of identity, their sense of being 'real women'. Queer women are often excluded from the social rewards that come with performing feminised labour in normative ways. Heterosexual desire is constructed as a natural bodily instinct, whereas queer desire is deemed unnatural. This means that queer forms of reproduction are continually stigmatised, unless they seek to mimic heterosexual ideals of the good life.

It is not simply the case that capital created gender exploitation in order to extract surplus value. Nor do divisions such as gender and race exist in order to split the working class. It is true that capitalists use the divisions within the working class to create competition between workers, to suppress wages and decrease the political capacities of the working class. But this fact in itself does little to explain why the divisions within the class are traced along the lines of race, gender, and other forms of hierarchical difference. Gender is not reducible to its function as a tool of the capitalist power to divide and rule. Every form of domination exceeds its merely functional deployment in capitalist value accumulation. We need to understand gender through particular forms of labour and subjectivity constructed through specific skills.

Possessive Individualism

Nancy Fraser and Linda Gordon suggest that in the nineteenth century, wage labour, previously seen as a form of dependence on an employer, was culturally re-coded as a sign of independence. White working-class men therefore came to appear as independent at the cost of other people – those who could not sell their labour power. Fraser and Gordon argue that masculine independence was created precisely through the form of waged work, in contrast to other subjects' perceived inability for independence.[18] As gender comes to be understood not as a social category but as something emanating from within, different types of subjectivity also come to be seen as inherently gendered. Agency and sovereignty are associated with masculine forms of subjectivity. In this context, sovereignty means the capacity to act as the ruler and owner of oneself, and to not be influenced by others or by 'irrational' emotion. This form of subjectivity can be understood as produced by the work of feminised subjects, who are lessening their own agency through the production of masculine sovereignty. The expectation that women perform deference and pliancy in relation to others is an invisible precondition for masculine subjectivity. As they have been able to access more power in capitalist societies, some women have been able to lay claim to this type of sovereignty, even if this claim is necessarily partial and unstable. This has occurred as a result of both feminist agitation and neoliberal forms of subjectivity, which on the surface emphasise choice and individual responsibility rather than traditional gender norms. But this individual responsibilisation quietly enforces gendered norms and forms of labour and simultaneously supports traditional family patterns, while seeming to allow for more agency for women.

The term possessive individualism, coined by C. B. Macpherson, is helpful for understanding the constitution of the hegemonic form of subjectivity under capitalism. Macpherson writes:

> Its possessive quality is found in its conception of the individual as essentially the proprietor of his own person or

63

capacities, owing nothing to society for them. The individual was seen neither as a moral whole, nor as part of a larger social whole, but as an owner of himself . . . The individual, it was thought, is free inasmuch as he is proprietor of his person and capacities.[19]

This is the hegemonic understanding of the subject under capitalism, and particularly under neoliberalism. But not everyone can inhabit possessive individualism to an equal degree. As the hegemonic subject position of capitalism, it both depends on and obscures other forms of subjectivity.

Affective individualism, possessive individualism, and the form of subjectivity assumed by the sale of labour power are all interrelated. These forms of individualism were all initiated by the bourgeoisie, but through the employment contact they came to influence working-class subjectivity as well. Possessive individualism can be understood in relation to the commodity form. Marx argues that the commodity appears to have an inherent value – hiding the social source of that value in relations of production. The commodity form makes invisible the labour it took to produce that commodity.[20] Possessive individualism is both a result and a precondition of the commodification of our capacity to labour, making this capacity appear as a thing belonging only to ourselves, and thus ours to sell for a wage. As with the case of the commodity form, the form of possessive individualism obscures the labour that goes into forming that very subject position.

The production of possessive individualism is not an automatic result of capitalist economic relations, but requires continual reaffirmation. As Fraser and Gordon show, independent subjectivity relies on gendered, classed, and racialised modes of dependence, which work as contrasts. These forms of dependence have been increasingly constructed as psychological traits rather than social positions.[21] The labour of affirming individuality becomes invisible through the form of possessive individualism, as the possessive individual appears to owe his capacities only to himself. He depends on a subject that does not inhabit possessive individualism. As Stephanie Coontz writes, 'Self-reliance and independence worked for *men* because *women* took care of dependence and obligation.'[22]

Emotional Altruism

In contrast to possessive individualism, then, feminised subjectivity is geared towards relational modes of being. Emotional reproduction is concerned with creating not merely feelings but with forming and maintaining social relationships. That is why the subject of emotional labour appears as the opposite of possessive individualism – it is a subject fundamentally concerned with building the relationality of society. Capitalist society creates a division between possessive individualism and emotional altruism – a split that maps onto gendered subjectivity. The labour of building affective relations becomes obscured in a world where the term work appears as the opposite of intimacy and emotion. The construction of possessive individualism is contrasted with the supposed emotionality of women. Individualism is built around self-possession and control of one's own emotional life. Femininity appears as lacking precisely the ability to be the master of one's own feelings.[23] It is understood as the condition of being the passive victim of emotional states rather than a sovereign individual.[24]

Individualism cannot subsist on its own, and not everyone is seen as a unique and self-sufficient individual. Our needs and vulnerabilities mean that we all depend on others. But this dependence becomes associated with those working to create and maintain relationships and sociality. Michèle Barrett and Mary McIntosh argue that under capitalism, the unit for 'self-support' is not the individual but the family.[25] Similarly, Cooper suggests that the constitution of sovereign liberal personhood depends on what it has disavowed, namely a form of subjectivity that creates community and dependence. Neoliberal politics celebrates individualism while depending on traditional family values. Cooper writes that neoliberalism posits 'an immanent ethics of virtue and a spontaneous order of family values that it expects to arise automatically from the mechanics of the free market system', adding that 'the nature of family altruism in some sense represents an internal exception to the free market, an immanent order of noncontractual obligations and inalienable services without which the world of contract would cease to function'.[26] The supposedly traditional world of family values is thus a precondition for the production of the forms of sovereign subjectivity on which liberalism depends and the construction of the notion of the market as a site of freedom through contractual models of obligation. Individualism cannot exist on its own, because people are vulnerable and rely on others to meet their need for care. Liberalism thus produces split forms of subjectivity – one hegemonic form and one that is necessary for that hegemony to persist.

The production of care is not the exclusive responsibility of women – it extends to other people in feminised positions. Christopher Carrington examines how gay and lesbian relationships tend to produce a more feminised partner whose main responsibility is the reproduction of the couple. Who comes to inhabit this position often depends on external factors such as employment and income. But the division of domestic labour within the couple becomes retrospectively justified and naturalised with reference to internal factors such as personality and proclivity for domestic work. This creates a hierarchy in which the person investing more time in reproductive work tends to be more dependent since they have less access to material resources and less time for participation in waged work.[27] Even in couples who present themselves as more egalitarian, then, the division of reproductive labour tends to be naturalised and attributed to the personality of the main caregiver.

The split subjectivity produced by capitalist economies creates a contradiction at the centre of many women's lives, as they are increasingly called upon to embody both of these forms of subjectivity. Under capitalism, Joan Acker writes, the worker is constructed as abstract and disembodied, lacking ties to other people.[28] However, feminised people are often tasked precisely with producing such ties. Women are increasingly called on to be workers and non-workers at the same time, both producing and obscuring social ties to others. Under neoliberalism, reduced state provision of reproductive services and the reprivatisation of much reproductive labour bind many women to reproductive work, both waged and unwaged.

The conflation of femininity and motherhood reinforces this relation, even as many women do not have children. Arlie Russell Hochschild writes:

> Because [women] are seen as members of the category from which mothers come, women in general are asked to look out for psychological needs more than men are. The world turns to women for mothering, and this fact silently attaches itself to many a job description.[29]

Given that they are often positioned as 'mothers' at work, feminised workers are clearly differentiated from the disembodied worker that Acker describes. Motherhood tends to attach itself even to those female workers who are not engaged in mothering work. Maya Gonzalez and Jeanne Neton argue that the naturalising assumption that all women are potential mothers forms the basis for women's low value on the labour market, as a potential cost of reproduction is turned into an expression of women's worthlessness.[30] This point is supported by the argument that the gender pay gap is in fact a 'motherhood penalty', as women are penalised for having children while it does not affect the earnings of men.[31]

While the capacity for motherhood appears to be the essential function of women's bodies, it is in fact unevenly distributed. Many women lack the ability to bear children. But motherhood itself should also be understood as a profoundly social category rather than just a natural capacity of bodies. As Roberts has shown, enslaved black women were excluded from the nineteenth-century construction of femininity. They were subjected to regimes of forced biological productivity while simultaneously being denied the right to relate to their children as kin.[32] This legacy is still present today. Racialised women have often been denied the status of motherhood based on the assumption that they are naturally unqualified for the 'spiritual' labour required to raise a child.[33] Instead, as Wages for Housework member Margaret Prescod shows, these women have been more valued for their waged reproductive labour, and are made to take on the work of 'mothering' white families while at the same time being made invisible as carers.[34] For many working-class women, especially women of colour and migrant women, the contradictory demands of waged work and domestic work are nothing new. Many of these women are engaged in the sector of waged reproductive work where the contradictory claims of various forms of subjectivity are less an issue than the lack of resources and time. This creates a situation where workers might become emotionally depleted from their caring labour in both waged and unwaged forms of work. These women might therefore experience the downsides of the exploitation of femininity without the rewards of being understood as a properly (white bourgeois) feminised subject.

The construction of labour power as a saleable commodity depends on various historically acquired capacities. According to Coontz, the construction of gender in capitalist economies 'meant specialization in one set of behaviours, skills, and feelings at the cost of suppressing others'.[35] Gendered skill is the knowledge of the body, enacted through repeated practices which bring gendered subjectivity into being. Kevin Floyd underscores that 'skill refers to nothing if not fully corporealized knowledge'.[36] The gendering of the self takes place through repetition of certain forms of activity. As we have seen, these activities become incorporated in the subject through habit and memory.[37] Work has often been explicitly associated with particular skills and capacities in ways which have contributed to the naturalisation of gender. Women's supposed lack of physical strength has been used as an argument to exclude women from many types of work, and these exclusions still operate despite many decades of legislation against workplace discrimination. With regards to traditionally masculine manual forms of waged labour, Cynthia Cockburn notes that the construction of skill depends on a process of exclusion of women from certain types of work. She writes that 'men have built their own relative bodily and technical strength by depriving women of theirs, and they have organised their occupation in such a way as to benefit from the differences they have constructed'.[38] While masculine work was typically seen as more skilled, women's skill appears to come from their inherent capacities for emotion and care.

Emotional skill is embodied knowledge, as supposedly preexisting inner states are communicated through words and bodily expressions – a process which simultaneously constitutes emotion through verbal and bodily communication. The construction of the body as having certain capacities is a way of enabling particular kinds of exploitation. This, as Selma James points out, also frees others from doing such labour, thus facilitating workers' exploitation by other workers.[39] Through the framework of gender complementarity, women's emotional skill is seen as something men lack. Barrett and McIntosh suggest that men have deskilled themselves in order to avoid responsibility for domestic work.[40] Because of men's emotional deskilling, they are excused from carrying out emotional labour while appearing as 'self-made' and not owing anything to the people who have cared for them. Women's supposedly natural emotional skill frees men from having to take responsibility for reproductive labour, simultaneously allowing them to enjoy the benefits of such work.[41] Masculinity appears as a lack of capacity for care, or an emotional ineptness, allowing men to ignore the needs of others and giving them the right to the care of women without having to reciprocate.[42] Men are therefore less likely to perceive and be influenced by the emotions of others. They have not had to train themselves in attending to the emotional needs of other people, and can therefore put their own needs first.

Natural Niceness

As women are generally tasked with the work of adapting to the emotional needs of others, the creation of good feeling, and the good life, becomes part of feminine skill for emotion management. Hochschild suggests that the creation of 'natural niceness' is a key feminised skill.[43] Feminised waged workers are hired for this skill – their supposedly natural personality – thus facilitating their exploitation in both waged and unwaged spheres. Feminised emotional labour relies on a set of bodily techniques, such as the ability to perform supposedly genuine smiles on demand. These techniques are taught to women in some professions. There seems to be some recognition that emotional capacities are learnt rather than spontaneous. But Hochschild notes that such training often draws on an imaginary of the home as the natural site for emotion and as a place of non-work.[44] Emotional skill is presented as something that feminised workers can simply transfer from their domestic lives to their workplaces – the home is imagined as an emotional sphere that can be expanded to include customers and co-workers.

This natural niceness depends on women's physical presentation of normative femininity. Much of women's consumption is often best conceived of as working on the body rather than a result of leisure time. The gendered body, while appearing as a natural given, is in fact the result of labour. Leopoldina Fortunati argues that this is part of the non-material reproductive labour that women do. The feminised body is part of the product of gendered labour. In this type of production, Fortunati writes:

> The raw materials and the means of work are incorporated within the female houseworker herself, within the individual. This implies that her non-material needs must not and cannot exist except as needs to satisfy the non-material needs of the male worker and her children. It also implies that she, apart from being labor-power is also a mere machine in the continuous cycle of non-material production. In this sense the female houseworker is capital's greatest technological invention. Thus, lipstick, powder, make-up in general are part of the process of non-material production, because they are added to the woman's body to effect a material change.[45]

Similarly, Federici and Nicole Cox write that a woman has to work on her body to reproduce her own labour power, and 'women well know the tyranny of this task, for a pretty dress and hairdo are conditions for their getting the job, whether on the marriage market or on the wage labor market'.[46] Processes of naturalisation of such capacities make them appear to be outside of the labouring subject's control. By naming this activity as work, the gendered body is denaturalised. It serves as a reminder of the constructedness of the capacities of the body.

Despite this skilled performance of feminised emotional labour across private and public spheres, femininity is seen as fundamentally passive. The naturalisation of feminine labour requires the skilful erasure of femininity as activity and as work. Women's naturalised skill in managing the emotional needs of others seems to reduce their own capacity for independence and sovereignty. The labour of care becomes read as an expression of the personality of the carer, inverting the dependency of others on this labour. According to Fraser and Gordon, 'The persons of female nurturers became saturated with the dependency of those for whom they care.'[47] They note that women's economic dependence on men historically has been constructed as a good type of dependency, but as more women have entered into waged work, all forms of dependence are increasingly characterised as psychological deficiency.[48] The feminised skill for emotional adaptability is increasingly constructed as undesirable and backwards, while remaining structurally necessary as a complement to possessive individualism.

Women's labour, especially that which is sexual or maternal, is conflated with their bodies and constructed as a natural instinct. This naturalisation is essential for the capitalist use of reproductive labour. The capacity for reproductive labour is turned into a natural quality of certain bodies whose function is primarily to carry out that labour. If it is not work, it is worthless economically, but also natural and therefore good. The naturalisation of feminised labour, and particularly emotional labour, not only makes that work appear as unskilled labour but also makes it invisible as labour. It is merely an eternal and unchangeable quality of feminine personalities. There is no separation between the work and the person; rather, the personality of the worker tends to subsume the work. Women's emotional labour is seen as a natural expression of their spontaneous feeling, something that is in turn used to further exploit this work. This apparent unskilled nature of emotional and bodily forms of labour is a central part of the general devaluation of reproduction. But gender, and femininity in particular, is the development of capacities rather than a lack of skill. According to James, race and gender function as imperatives 'to develop and acquire certain capabilities at the expense of all others. Then these acquired capabilities are taken to be our nature, fixing our functions for life, and fixing also the quality of our mutual relations.'[49] The apparent deskilling and invisibility of gendered labour is itself a skilled vanishing act which becomes part of the acquired capacities of gender.

The Good Life

The labour of creating good feeling is seen as a natural aspect of women's personalities. This work is also the work of creating an emotional investment in good feeling itself – taking pleasure in niceness and learning to desire it. In that way, creating good feeling becomes a way of creating an emotional investment in the good life – normative ideals for what a life should look like. Consciously turning away from the good life can be a difficult task – one that leads to social exclusion and punishment.[50] It is through emotional investment in the good life that we come to desire certain relationships and things over others. The suburban family home becomes a symbol of the good life, and we invest emotionally in achieving it. We imagine it as the sphere of love – a true love that can offer meaning to our lives. Even for those who have an intellectual critique of these values, it can be hard to rid oneself of the desire for this way of life. The emotional labour that women perform – by creating niceness and emotional attachments to a particular form of life – is a very effective way of ensuring the reproduction of society as we know it. We come to desire a certain way of life and the forms of labour that come with it, even if the labour itself feels bad.

As Fortunati writes, it is considered natural that men consume love, whereas women's 'generous' personalities are productive of love.[51] The construction of women as generous

73

also implies that for women, love is its own reward – to perform the work of love is a sufficient source of pleasure, so that no other remuneration is needed. While women are the main producers of love, their work is simultaneously paid for by the love they receive from their partners. Federici notes that women are expected to express gratitude towards their male partners, as 'they have given us the opportunity to express ourselves as women (i.e., to serve them)'.[52] Love becomes the reward for desiring the right things – desiring a life based on gendered forms of labour and heterosexual complementarity.

It is the legitimacy of normative heterosexuality, compared to sexual relations outside the heterosexual work ethic, that binds women to their work. It offers the emotional reward of being a properly gendered subject. This legitimacy produces emotional investment in the institution of heterosexual monogamy, which, as Lauren Berlant suggests, maintains the association between the good life and heterosexuality.[53] The productive force of love, then, rather than just the punitive logic of violence, maintains hierarchy and exploitation. Through investment in the good life of heterosexuality, many women also participate in their own exploitation. We all have certain attachments in the world as it is, and these investments are a core aspect of emotional reproduction.

Women tend to do more emotional labour than men, and they generally do it in a specifically feminised way. Feminised forms of emotional labour often involve smiling, showing deference, and smoothing over any upset feelings. Women have a weaker socio-economic position in society, and are socialised to privilege the emotional needs of others over their own. Hochschild writes that women generally have a more restricted access to economic resources, and therefore tend to make a resource out of emotion.[54] However, this resource is one that implies the subject's subordination to others rather than a thing that can be owned or fully controlled. Through their emotional labour, feminised emotion workers also enhance the status of the people around them, often by showing that those people are more important than the worker herself. This production of other people's status means that women's emotional labour also reproduces their own lack of status. The exploitation of women's capacities for work continually reinforces their subordinated position.

According to Federici, women are made to service men 'physically, emotionally, and sexually, to raise his children, mend his socks, patch up his ego when it is crushed by the work and the social relations (which are relations of loneliness) that capital has reserved for him'.[55] Emotional reproduction is a central condition for the continuation of capitalist labour relations, as it seeks to compensate for the harms of capitalism. This has particular effects on those who have been made responsible for the needs of others. In Mariarosa Dalla Costa's words, the heterosexual woman must try to emulate the image of the ' "heroic mother and happy wife" whose sexual identity is pure sublimation, whose function is essentially that of receptacle for other people's emotional expression, who is the cushion of the familial antagonism'.[56] Women are required to perform happiness while simultaneously being on the receiving end of negative emotions – a characteristic that is familiar for those who are engaged in reproductive service jobs. But the individualisation of emotional labour within the family, which is a precondition for capitalist emotional reproduction, also makes this work more burdensome for women. The people cared for in the family must believe that they 'can only be reproduced by this one woman in one particular privatized individualized situation'.[57] She is always on call in order to ensure the continuous reproduction of her loved ones. Her continual presence serves to soothe tensions and offers the promise that care is available when needed.[58]

Femininity prescribes that emotion should primarily be used in the service of others. Women's skill in emotional adaptability tends to position them as inherently responsive to the needs of other people. Hochschild points to women's tendency to act as 'conversational cheerleaders', enhancing the social performance of others.[59] In Pamela Fishman's study of conversational patterns within heterosexual couples, she found that female participants were much more likely to actively demonstrate that they were listening, continuously affirming their partner's opinions and choice of conversational topics.[60] Small but reiterated gestures of support that women make are thus used to perpetuate their subordination. Men use the confidence they gain from their female partner's emotional support to position themselves as superior to their partner.[61] This does not mean that women are to blame for their own oppression, but neither are they passive victims of gender oppression and exploitation. Rather, women tend to actively participate in the continual reproduction of a reality based on gender hierarchy.

Emotion workers are participants in creating social realities, even when those realities continually marginalise them. Women are also actively working to erase any signs of emotional labour – that is, they actively disguise their own labour under the banners of niceness and natural femininity. Emotional labour is an invisible background condition that enables more visible forms of labour and production to take place. It is an 'unseen effort, which, like housework, does not quite count as labor but is nevertheless crucial to getting other things done'.[62] This effort is a precondition for emotional reproduction, as well as for the continued reproduction of gender.

The invisibility of emotional labour is premised on a differential valuation of emotion based on gender. If women's emotional expression is visible as emotion, it is because men's emotional expressions tend to be interpreted as a statement of fact. Hochschild writes that when men express anger, 'it is deemed "rational" or understandable anger, anger that indicates not weakness of character but deeply held conviction'. In contrast, 'women's feelings are not seen as a response to real events but as reflections of themselves as "emotional" women'.[63] While women perform more of the invisible work of attending to the feelings of others, they are nonetheless deemed to be excessively emotional themselves. There is a circular association of femininity and emotion in which femininity is devalued because of its connection with emotionality while emotion becomes devalued when coded as feminine. This serves to empower those expressing the right kind of feelings while marginalising those who are thought to express improper, excessive, and feminised emotions. As men's expressions of feeling are coded as rational rather than emotional, they have a greater claim to constructing a generally accepted view of the world. While women work harder to maintain social relations, men have greater control over the content of the world view created in those interactions. Women thus often work to affirm a construction of the world that persistently subordinates them. This serves the reproduction of gender hierarchy and women's subordinate position, especially within heterosexual relationships.

Hochschild points out that the fact that women tend to form intimate connections with men differentiates gendered oppression from hierarchies based on race or class.[64] This intimacy explains the primacy of emotional labour within gendered oppression, as this labour creates the social relations that perpetuate gendered hierarchy. While racialised and classed oppression and exploitation primarily play out at work or in public, gender is continually reproduced through intimate family relations. Emotional labour has been increasingly commodified since women started to enter waged work in greater numbers, but gendered oppression at work is distinctly shaped by relations formed in the private sphere. This gives heterosexual gender relations a distinct character, as the subordinated are tasked with forming intimate bonds of love with their oppressors and adapt their seemingly authentic emotional lives to the needs of those who subordinate them. Hochschild writes that since 'men and women do try to love one another . . .

the very closeness of the bond they accept calls for some disguise of subordination'.[65] Emotional labour, then, not only reproduces more general forms of gendered exploitation and oppression but also presents oppression as love.

Men tend to feel more entitled to their partner's nurturance than women do. This runs contrary to the received knowledge that women are more emotionally demanding in intimate relationships. According to this understanding of heterosexual love, men express their love differently, and it is unfair of women to demand full reciprocity. This idea mobilises the trope of men as emotionally inexpressive – what Stephanie Shields calls the paradigm of masculinity as self-control.[66] Men can reinforce their power by withholding emotional expression.[67] This also means that women often have to rely on other women for emotional support. According to Tamsin Wilton, heterosexual women's friendships tend to function as support systems that serve to uphold male dominance by naturalising men's lack of emotional reciprocity. Such support systems aim to minimise the emotional harms of heterosexual relationships without challenging the source of that harm.[68] Friendship can therefore function as a source of emotional reproduction, which serves to shore up the very relationships that continually marginalise those friendships and posits them as less important than romantic love and family bonds.

The fact that women are generally more trained in handling the feelings of both self and others does not imply that men are less emotional. But emotions are expressed, perceived, and interpreted in gendered ways. Men and women also tend to specialise in different aspects of the same job. Hochschild writes that male and female flight attendants are partly doing different jobs, as men tend to specialise in more physical tasks whereas women are assigned the work of creating good feeling.[69] Women joining the waged labour force to an increasing degree does not necessarily mean that they have become part of the masculine culture of work. Rather, feminised labour has become increasingly commodified. Gender and status are not pre-given in the labour process but rather continually enforced through gendered agency. Gender is produced by the active participation of workers in certain tasks and through their relations to other people. In Hochschild's study, male flight attendants were less likely to be the targets of negative emotion. Customers were much more likely to unburden their negative emotion, such as anger and distress, on female service workers. Shiloh Whitney writes that emotional labour does not necessarily create a good feeling in the customer but often invites the customer to offload negative feeling onto the worker.[70] Women are expected to show deference to customers, especially male customers, and to respond to abuse with a smile.[71] The person starting a job requiring emotional labour does not enter it with a pre-social or authentic form of subjectivity which is then commercialised. Instead, unwaged and seemingly private but already exploitative forms of labour constitute the feminised subject before she enters the waged labour force.

These processes are part of the production of gender as such. Whitney notes that women are 'constructed as non-intentional, non-agentic, or nonauthoritative', as agency is often constructed as an opposite of 'being emotional', while emotional labour at the same time reinforces other people's capacity to act.[72] These forms of labour are processes in which dominated subjects participate rather than passively endure. For example, Carin Holmberg found that the women interviewed in her study of heterosexual relationships were more likely to express a high valuation of traditionally masculine traits than were their male partners.[73] Feminised forms of labour function to decrease the degree of perceived agency that labouring subjects possess, as their emotional expression is understood not as making something happen in the world but merely as a reflection of their own susceptibility to emotion.[74] Conversely, those who have their emotional needs catered to come to understand themselves as socially valued and having the power to change things. It is through interactions with less powerful others that some people come to inhabit sovereign subjectivity.

But not all forms of emotional expression decrease individual sovereignty. Perhaps the most masculinised of all emotions, anger is often an expression of power and entitlement. Anger creates a position of agency. The masculine emotional labour of performing anger is not reproductive in the sense of contributing to the wellbeing of other people. Yet it might serve to maintain certain hierarchies which reproduce the current organisation of society. Masculinity is produced not only through physical or intellectual labour but also through the typically feminised work of emotion management. Feminised workers are mainly made to absorb anger and frustration without necessarily externalising it and displacing it onto someone else. Masculinity, on the other hand, works through the displacement of anger onto others, as it has a seeming monopoly on aggression and violence.

Naturalised gender positions are continually reproduced through bodily techniques which create particular emotional states and relationships. Hochschild's flight attendants performed various versions of the idealised femininity of the white bourgeoisie. These draw simultaneously on sexiness and care, producing an ideal mother–girlfriend figure who is constructed as both emotionally and sexually available to (male) customers. As Hochschild puts it,

> female flight attendants are expected to *enact* two leading roles of Womanhood: the loving wife and mother (serving food, tending the needs of others) and the glamorous 'career woman' (dressed to be seen, in contact with strange men, professional and controlled in manner, and literally very far from home).[75]

Emotional labour is built on the performance of a limited but flexible set of gendered norms which can respond to differing emotional needs. Because women are expected to respond to a number of needs in others, it is essential to femininity that it can contain multiple and sometimes contradictory versions of womanhood. Hochschild shows how flight attendants developed various bodily techniques to perform femininity, from 'sexual queen' to 'Cub Scout den mother'.[76] These forms of femininity are highly limited and constricted by normative patterns, yet they afford female workers some flexibility in using different types of femininity to achieve various ends. This gives female workers some agency to act through femininity, but it does very little to undo gendered emotional labour as such.

Contradictory Requirements

While post-war European and North American ideals of the housewife produced relatively homogeneous experiences among women in the core capitalist countries, as many women were unwaged reproductive workers, neoliberal society has given rise to increasing stratification among women of different classes. Many women have achieved prominence in masculinised spheres of work, such as business, politics, and law. The second-wave feminist movement won legal rights and increased economic and sexual independence for women. Yet gender hierarchy persists. The concept of emotional reproduction, and its attendant forms of subjectivity, can help us to think through patterns of gendered power and labour. Emotional reproduction can account for the persistence of gendered differentiation in contemporary capitalist society, even as the dual-earner family model has become the norm.

As femininity is simultaneously rewarded and devalued, professional women might find themselves in a double bind. In many cases these women are pressured to distance themselves from reproductive labour and traditional femininity while at the same time preserving some aspects of it so as not to appear as gender deviants.[77] For these women, gender becomes a balancing act which often involves displacing the devalued labour of femininity onto other women. The disavowal of traditional femininity is mapped onto race, so that women of colour and migrant women are constructed as inhabiting a more backwards type of femininity compared to the supposedly modern and sovereign subjectivity that white bourgeois women can claim.[78] Sara Farris shows how this has been translated into the political demand, from both right-wing politicians and some feminist organisations, that migrant women should be compelled to perform waged work in order to escape their supposed backwardness. However, these women are made to engage in the sectors which white women are seeking to escape, such as care and cleaning.[79] Having a career becomes the test of modern (or masculine) subjectivity compared to the devalued position of traditional (feminine) wagelessness. This ignores the fact that women of colour have historically been more likely to do waged work than white women.[80] Even when passing the test of having a job, migrant women of colour are often stuck with a devalued form of femininity because of their persistent association with seemingly unskilled forms of care work.

Neoliberal society has brought with it an increased valuation of social flexibility. Flexibility has often been understood as detraditionalising gender, making gender expression appear less rigid. But such detraditionalisation does not necessarily mean that gender hierarchies disappear. Rather, they are reconstituted in new ways.[81] Contemporary economies continue to rely on hierarchical divisions within the workforce as well as the availability of devalued reproductive labour.

Their increased participation in the waged labour force has enabled white, middle-class or bourgeois women to achieve a greater degree of power and independence. These women might have their own needs met to a higher extent because they can become the carriers of valued, high-skilled labour power. It has also enabled them, at least to some degree, to refuse the burden of reproductive labour, often by partially outsourcing it to designated reproductive workers. In capitalist society, reproductive labour is deemed incompatible with sovereign subjectivity because this type of labour privileges the needs of others. Such needs, rather than individual will, become the orienting force of this labouring subject. Inhabiting sovereignty therefore means refusing the work of reproducing others. The fact that some women have been able to lay claim to sovereignty and agency has not done away with the distinction between those who perform reproductive labour and those who do not. It has merely redrawn the lines of these groups, allowing for some flexibility for a highly select group of women. These women might themselves struggle to fully inhabit possessive individualism since it is constructed as the opposite of the femininity they were often raised to perform, and they risk being punished if they step too far from normative femininity. Professional women may sometimes feel the need to emphasise that they are mothers first and foremost, and put the needs of others before their own, in order to inhabit the right form of womanhood.

Feminised subjectivity is itself not internally coherent. We have seen how contemporary capitalist society produces contradictory demands on women, but femininity has never had a simple or stable meaning. Federici argues that femininity in the transition to capital was reconfigured from an association with uncontrollable sexuality to signifiers such as docility and chastity.[82] But femininity has retained some of its contradictory meanings, which makes it useful as a technique for extracting labour and controlling workers. As Melissa Wright has shown in her study of women factory work in China and Mexico, the coexistence of several versions of femininity means that different aspects of femininity can be mobilised in ways that increase gendered domination and exploitation – women are seen as more docile and dexterous than men, but also as natural and unskilled physicality in need of constant control as the unruly feminine body constantly threatens to disrupt the flow of production.[83] The construction of feminine passivity and docility is unstable and flexible. This flexibility itself enables the hyper-exploitation of women workers, as they become subject to exploitation inside and outside of the formal workplace. It also makes them vulnerable to violence, both inside and outside waged work. Gendered subjectivities emerge as the effects of gendered forms of production and control. In places of work, in both the home and the formal economy, gendered subjectivity is simultaneously presupposed and reproduced.

This flexibility does not necessarily challenge the naturalisation of gender. Instead, people are often able to fit a more flexible gender presentation within their conceptualisation of a gender binary.[84] Various forms of femininity can coexist and sometimes come into contradiction without undoing the continual devaluation of what is deemed feminine. A more flexible construction of gendered work, where women are not only housewives but waged workers, does not necessarily threaten this devaluation. As more women have entered waged work over the past decades, they have become a source of cheap labour power rather than just of unwaged services – both are expressions of the devaluation of reproductive work. This devaluation is connected to the unwaged nature of much reproductive labour, which remains even as we have seen a trend towards commodification of some reproductive work over the past decades. Nona Glazer notes that this trend is not unilinear, and that there is a significant degree of flexibility in the reproductive sphere, where various forms of reproductive work tend to shift back and forth between waged and unwaged spheres according to the cycles of capitalist investment and disinvestment and the expansion and retraction of state services. She suggests that women are supposed to act as 'sponges' that can absorb unwaged and waged work.[85] Femininity is constructed as a form of receptivity whose flexibility consists of the capacity to adapt to the changing needs of others, combining waged and unwaged work in ways that fit the needs of the family, the market, and the state.

The neoliberal and flexible construction of femininity might thus imply the increasing exploitation of (some) women across the waged and unwaged spheres. While women's participation in the waged labour force temporally limits their unwaged work, and necessitates the use of commodified reproductive services, many women are nonetheless participating in the unwaged care of family and friends. Often this means that they have less time for themselves, for rest and for reproducing their own labour power. The reproductive labour these women perform is integrated in naturalised understandings of femininity and care in order for them to be de- and recommodified according to the needs of various people and institutions. Women's flexibility becomes the work of responding to these needs, accepting previously waged work back into the private sphere according to the current organisation of state-provided services, and the always partial and limited forms of commodified reproductive services that the market provides.

Flexibility, then, means different things for different subjects within neoliberal society. For feminised subjects, it means the ability to reabsorb the work that has been relegated to the private sphere after the cuts to public reproductive services, as well as absorbing the stresses and shocks of an increasingly precarious economic position for many people. Federici writes:

> Women have been the shock absorbers of economic globalization, having had to compensate with their work for the deteriorating economic conditions produced by the liberalization of the world economy and the state's increasing disinvestment in the reproduction of the workforce.[86]

As in the sphere of waged labour, the notion of flexibility tends to have negative connotations for those who are exploited. Flexibility often means being able to respond to the demands of the boss. For bourgeois men, neoliberal constructions of flexible subjectivity might entail more desirable forms of mobility and reflexivity – the ability to change according to the subject's own desires. This form of flexibility, while presented as the undoing of social hierarchy and norms, is in fact more available to some.[87] Rebecca Selberg, in her study of nurses in a hospital deploying neoliberal management techniques, notes that some female nurses are allowed upward mobility, insofar as they can inhabit a form of youthful, modern energy and individualism that is seen as desirable within these regimes of the self. Liberal feminists consider this a sign of the undoing of gendered norms and the creation of a less strict gender division of labour. But this does nothing to ease the burden of those women who are left doing the devalued and often invisible work of caring for patients.[88] In fact, neoliberal 'rationality' in the public sector tends to exacerbate the pressures of these positions through regimes of austerity and outsourcing. Liberal feminism has often simply neglected issues of reproduction while celebrating women's entrance into management positions.

True Feeling

In some accounts of emotional labour, alienation is presented as the main problem with this type of work. Emotional labour is seen as problematic because women become alienated from their supposedly more authentic feelings in ways that cause distress and decrease their real emotional capacities. But feminised subjects are not necessarily harmed by the practices of emotional labour. This form of work is ambivalent in its effect on both working subjects and on recipients of care. We should be wary of deriving moral or political value from the pleasures that some people performing emotional labour can get from their work. Such pleasures do not necessarily make labour practices better or less exploitative. In fact, people can derive pleasure from practices that are limiting and harmful to themselves and others. A case in point is the pleasure that heterosexual women derive from their participation in intimate coupledom, which is a source of exploitation as well as rewards. As Berlant writes, we often have optimistic emotional investments in the very things that hurt us.[89] Berlant suggests that women, while routing their own emotional needs through the needs of others, might also derive some pleasure from receiving their 'own value back not only in the labour of recognition she performs but in the sensual spectacle of its impact. In this discursive field, women's emotional labour places them at the centre of the story of what counts as life.'[90] Some subjects can derive pleasure from the proper performance of femininity often embedded in emotional labour practices. Conversely, men who are performing traditionally feminised emotional labour might have to deal with the cognitive and emotional stress of combining their work with their investment in masculinity.[91] For feminised subjects, emotional labour often involves the pleasure of expressing (and thus reproducing) a supposedly authentic femininity.

This close association of emotion and subjectivity means that it is difficult to construe emotional labour as discrete tasks which can be codified in a job description. Because it is deeply naturalised and seen as inherent in the personality of the worker, emotional labour often cannot achieve the status as a saleable product separable from its seller. This is part of the reason why emotional labour is often not a service in itself but rather an invisible component of other services. As Steve Taylor and Melissa Tyler argue, there are 'aspects of women's work which take place outside of formal, contractual relations of exchange, yet upon which formal contractual relations of commodity exchange depend'. Emotional labour becomes compulsory altruism.[92] This is valuable for capitalist production, which is based on requiring workers to do more work than they are paid for.

Gendered exploitation is thus integrated in capitalist labour markets. This often plays out in the seemingly insignificant interactions between men and women, both at home and in waged work. Mariarosa Dalla Costa writes that 'between men and women power as its right *commands* sexual affection and intimacy'.[93] Just as capitalist power is the power to command labour, so gender is the power to command the labour of intimacy. This command of gendered labour is not merely external. Gender functions through the internalisation of the command for emotional and reproductive labour. The requirement to sacrifice oneself is at the core of normative femininity. Not only are women trained to sacrifice themselves for others, they are also encouraged to derive pleasure from this work.[94] The labour of gender demands that the worker not only performs the work but enjoys it. The work of love also comes with an imperative to remodel subjectivity itself in the image of this work.

The feminised working subject is disciplined by this imperative to enjoy work or suffer the individualised blame for failing to enjoy it. As Federici writes, if you do not like it, 'it is your problem, your failure, your guilt, and your abnormality'.[95] Through notions of sacrifice, femininity functions as a disciplinary tool for extracting more work. Emotional labour in particular should ideally be infinite in nature. The psychic structure of self-sacrifice remains powerful especially for those women who are engaged in care work and who are emotionally invested in being a good person, that is, a good woman.[96] The compulsory nature of much emotional labour, and care more generally, is particularly evident when care is decommodified. When state provision of reproductive services is cut, or when capitalist investment retreats from unprofitable forms of reproductive labour, family and friends are often made to perform the work of care in an unpaid capacity. The emotional attachment to the person in need of care, as well as the feminised imperative to perform emotional labour, might compel women to perform care for family or friends even when it limits their capacity to care for themselves.

4

Feminist Emotions

They say it is love. We say it is unwaged work.
They call it frigidity. We call it absenteeism.
Every miscarriage is a work accident.
Homosexuality and heterosexuality are both working condi-
tions . . . but homosexuality is workers' control of production,
not the end of work.
More smiles? More money. Nothing will be so powerful in
destroying the healing virtues of a smile.
Neuroses, suicides, desexualization: occupational diseases of
the housewife.

—Silvia Federici, 'Wages against Housework'

In order for resistance and confrontation to become possible, feminist subjectivity must move from one form of emotional practice to another. The negative emotional states associated with femininity, such as fear, guilt, and anxiety, can change their meaning through the constitution of collective subjectivity. This shift does not necessarily imply more positive emotional states. Feminist movements can make use of bad feelings. These feelings, however, must be collectivised in order to become useful. Alison Jaggar's concept of outlaw emotions can help us think about how this shift can happen. Jaggar observes that emotions, while socially constituted, are not fully determined by social structures in the sense that everyone feels the same thing. Those who 'pay a disproportionately high price for maintaining the status quo' are more likely to experience outlaw emotions – that is, feelings that are not condoned in a certain social situation.[1] Some of the people who experience oppression and exploitation might begin to feel angry rather than scared or resigned. In Arlie Russell Hochschild's terms, such emotions do not pay the social 'debt' owed by particular individuals.[2] When isolated, the individual experiencing outlaw emotions might be experienced as insane or emotionally disturbed – as a person whose emotional practices are out of sync with the expectations and pressures of normative social bonds.[3] Silvia Federici writes that 'many women have rebelled and are rebelling in this way. They are called "insane". In reality, they are women who have not found any other way of refusing being exploited except by putting themselves out of use, out of being used.'[4] In reading the 'insanity' of women as a tacit form of refusal, non-normative or undesirable feelings can become 'politically (because epistemologically) subversive'.[5] Feeling differently is also a way of knowing differently, and knowing that the world could be different. Forming a collective feminist subjectivity, which is also a collective of feeling, allows people to find communal ways of refusing. Such refusals seek to turn the effects of exploitation outward rather than internalising them.

One way of refusing was explored by the Geneva Wages for Housework group Collectif l'Insoumise. Their practice included direct actions, occupations, collective fare dodging, and prisoner solidarity. It also included a more direct appeal to the emotional elements of struggle, as the group focused on collective forms of organisation for 'bad' and 'angry' mothers. Refusing the glorification of motherhood as self-sacrifice, Collectif l'Insoumise celebrated the mothers 'whom society and right-thinking people consider bad because they don't do exactly what the state, the family, the Church, and the cops want them to do'. These women 'don't have the smell of resignation and sacrifice; instead, they have the good scent of revolt and freedom!'[6] The recuperation of anger as a political practice allowed Collectif l'Insoumise to move beyond individual fear of punishment for risky behaviour and outlaw emotions.

They used their writings to inspire collective feelings such as anger, frustration, and discontent. Refusing to be 'good' mothers – that is, refusing the work demanded by the ideal of self-sacrificing, white, bourgeois motherhood – the group sought to mobilise those women who wanted more for themselves. They called on 'Those who are trying to live as they like, Those who complain everywhere, at unemployment, at taxes, at the job . . . Those who don't live only for their kid.'[7]

Their practice was not to foster 'better' feelings than the resentment they already experienced but to mobilise those feelings in a way that amplified their liberatory possibilities. Outlaw emotions, Jaggar argues, are not in themselves subversive but can be put to use in revolutionary political projects when integrating revolutionary values. They are appropriate to radical politics when characteristic of a society in which human suffering and exploitation is lessened, or is conducive to establishing such a society.[8] She suggests that emotions have a valuable epistemological function, as 'conventionally inexplicable emotions may lead us to make subversive observations'.[9]

Outlaw emotions are essential to the refusal of emotional reproduction. Emotional labour can be described as the work to suppress or hide such emotions in order to foster more socially appropriate feelings. The collective feminist practice of anger is a way of refusing feminised emotional labour. While anger is a common state in more masculine emotional displays, it is the feeling that must be managed and suppressed in feminised forms of emotional labour, as well as absorbed from others, in order to create a spirit of niceness.[10] While the recuperation of anger within a feminist project might seem to simply affirm a more masculine emotional style, it is essential to the refusal of feminised emotional labour. This does not imply that anger is the only emotional state worth amplifying, or that more feminised emotions are to be discarded. Rather, we should recognise the political power of anger when put to use by those who are exploited and oppressed, who are expected to respond to violence with compliancy. This also entails a more equitable access to various emotional states and moving away from the constitution of a supposedly authentic gendered being through emotional practices. In this way, the broadening of the feelings available to feminised subjects might point towards a horizon of gender abolition. A different and wider emotional practice could open the potential for a different, non-feminised subject without affirming the emotional practice of possessive individualism.

Anger is an ambivalent feeling, often used to oppressive ends, not only by men but also by women against other women. As emotion is contextual in its nature, we must pay careful attention to the political nuances of anger. In her essay 'A Note on Anger', Marilyn Frye suggests that female anger is not an outlaw emotion per se. Women are allowed to express anger within their 'proper domain' – that of the kitchen.[11] It is when women's anger exceeds the privatised reproductive sphere that it becomes threatening to the emotional ordering of the world. Collective practices of anger have the potential to challenge the status quo. As Audre Lorde observes, 'Every woman has a well-stocked arsenal of anger potentially useful against those oppressions, personal and institutional, which brought that anger into being. Focused with precision it can become a powerful source of energy serving progress and change.'[12] Lorde argues for the use of anger to resist white, heterosexual, bourgeois femininity, which also perpetuates the oppression of other women. This femininity is constituted through practices of niceness that seek to obscure conflict and hierarchy while at the same time perpetuating them.

Yet, anger can be dampened by individualised feelings of fear and guilt. Federici remarks that one of the main obstacles for women to refuse this work is 'the fear of being seen as bad women rather than as workers on strike'.[13] Similarly, Lorde writes:

For women raised to fear, too often anger threatens annihilation. In the male construct of brute force, we were taught that our lives depended upon the good will of patriarchal power. The anger of others was to be avoided at all costs, because there was nothing to be learned from it but pain, a judgment that we had been bad girls, come up lacking, not done what we were supposed to do. And if we accept our powerlessness, then of course any anger can destroy us.[14]

But there is no need to accept powerlessness, as women are in fact not powerless. The emotional cost of being seen as a 'bad' woman can be resisted collectively. Through the refusal of work, women display their power. This can be through small acts of defiance, such as when the female flight attendants in Hochschild's study stop smiling or refuse the additional work of presenting their smiles as 'genuine'.[15] Through the escalation of collective anger, this could turn into Shulamith Firestone's 'dream action for the women's movement', the smile boycott.[16] Or in the Wages for Housework formulation, this could mean only smiling when we are paid for it, thus undermining the supposed authenticity of women's emotional display. Hochschild notes that women who do not smile tend to be read as being angry.[17] This is especially true of black women, who are frequently seen as angry and threatening.[18] Failure to show positive emotion, then, is automatically understood as anger. This clarifies the link between anger and refusal, as refusal to produce niceness immediately marks one as emotionally deviant.

Wages for Housework authors interpret many types of behaviour as forms of refusal of feminised work. Individual acts such as divorce and shoplifting, and states such as frigidity and depression, are all read as symptoms of a more generalised disenchantment with the ideological power and emotional investments of gendered work. Through refusing to perform work, especially that which is normally not seen as work, a feminist collective subject could lay bare a source of power that was previously unknown. However, refusal can take many different expressions and is dependent on the kind of labour demanded of particular subjects. Wilmette Brown reads black women's higher birth rates as a form of refusal of the racist attempts to discipline black women's sexuality into normative, white, and bourgeois forms of reproductive labour.[19] There are thus multiple and context-specific ways of resisting the dominant reproductive order.

The Wages for Housework strategy of refusal can also be understood as a refusal of the individualising and isolating aspects of emotional reproduction. Wages for Housework authors take aim at the conditions of reproducing labour power, which under capitalist conditions are necessarily isolating. Refusing to reproduce oneself and others as labour power also means opening the possibility for other forms of sociality. Kathi Weeks reads feminist refusal in terms of diffusion of affective capacities, which are currently narrowly situated in the sphere of the family and romantic love, and increasingly in the sphere of waged work.[20] This opens a broader emotional horizon and challenges the privatisation of feeling. Seeing the refusal of labour as a way of inventing forms of collective care takes us beyond the binary framework of refusal versus valorisation of reproductive work. Refusal instead becomes a tool for the valorisation of a different form of life.

In the Wages for Housework writings, refusal is a strategy of denaturalisation. Refusing the work of love also means cutting the link between womanhood and reproduction, something the valorisation and visibilisation of domestic labour cannot do. Through refusing to work for love, women simultaneously undermine the apparent naturalness of femininity. In 'Wages against Housework', Federici argues that we must *refuse that work as the expression of our nature*, and therefore . . . refuse precisely the female role that capital has invented for us'.[21] Through a feminist antiwork politics, femininity stops being functional to capital. Denaturalising gender means that we can begin to do what we want rather than what the imposition of gendered labour dictates.

But as the Tri-Veneto Wages for Housework Committee noted in 1974, 'The price we women pay for this refusal is high. Men block our struggle, they blackmail us, they beat us, they kill us.'[22] In order to protect women from violence, feminist collectivities need anger, but also solidarity, as the basis for an alternative form of sociality. Solidarity depends on the development of alternative emotional practices. Wages for Housework writings and activism encouraged the emotional practice of solidarity with other women. In *The Power of Women and the Subversion of the Community*, Mariarosa Dalla Costa argues that solidarity exists not for defence but for attack, for coming 'together with other women, not only as neighbors and friends but as workmates and anti-workmates'.[23] This means that solidarity relies not only on empathy, as a feeling-with more vulnerable others, but an unlearning of conventional emotional responses that obstruct coalition-building. In line with the Wages for Housework political inversion, through which those seen as the most powerless are re-described as powerful, there is a need for a similar reinterpretation of emotional practices. We can think of the Wages for Housework writers' strong identification with the frequently dismissed position of the 'backward' housewife, but also their insistence of building coalitions between housewives, low-paid service workers, women on welfare, and sex workers. Solidarity can act as a check on women's anger and resentment against those in more marginal positions, as in when housewives display anger against women on welfare. Federici writes of such housewives, 'Her anger is an immediate expression of her envy for the fact that she, the housewife, is not able to refuse that portion of her work and does not have some money of her own.'[24] The housewife's emotional state is an example of negative solidarity – of turning bad feeling against those who are more oppressed rather than against the oppressor. But the feeling of anger towards those who are more stigmatised is reinterpreted as a feeling of envy of those who are able to refuse. The position that is seemingly more marginalised is recast as enviable. This emotional response of individualised anger has to be unlearned in order for feelings of collective anger and power to develop.

Emotional Antagonisms

In the short verse cited at the beginning of this chapter, Wages for Housework stage an antagonistic relation between a 'they' that mystifies these conditions and a 'we' that reveals seemingly disconnected incidents as part of the collective situation of feminised subjects. Neuroses and miscarriages are no longer private misfortunes but rather occupational diseases and work accidents. Smiles will not come for free anymore since they are expressions not of love but of a labour practice. The struggle for wages fundamentally changes the meaning of those smiles, and even destroys their healing virtues. Women's supposed frigidity is turned into a moment of struggle against sexual labour by being renamed absenteeism. The Wages for Housework writings are full of examples of how women's expressions of discontent with their conditions are typically individualised and therefore need to be reinterpreted and reinserted into a political framework of resistance. Federici observes that 'we are seen as nagging bitches, not workers in struggle'.[25] Wages for Housework reinterpret this 'nagging', so that the women engaged in it can understand themselves as already participating in the emotional practices of this collective 'we' and ready to take their hitherto individualised complaint to a new level of collective antagonism.

This reinterpretation is necessary to move from a description of the conditions of housework to a call to action. Federici contends that

> from now on, we want money for every moment of it, so that we can refuse some of it and eventually all of it. Nothing can be more effective than to show that our female virtues have already a calculable money value: until today only for capital, increased in the measure that we were defeated, but from now on, against capital, for us, in the measure that we organize our power.[26]

Articulating that capital is the main enemy allows Wages for Housework to claim for themselves a pivotal role in working-class struggle and stage an epistemological, emotional, and political inversion – what appeared as the most intimate (the smile, the miscarriage) is now the most political. It is from the experience of defeat, oppression, and exploitation that a new political and emotional project can arise. The old acceptance of the state of things is turned into a desire for a different world.

This project also challenges the established political truisms of the left. Selma James's writings are exemplary in creating interventions in left political discourse in which the seemingly marginal becomes central. This move produces a redefinition of the working class, in which those excluded from waged work become essential political actors in the struggle against capital. For James, the aim of the feminist struggle must be to build enough power to make men join the feminist anti-capitalist revolution: 'Now we demand unity on our terms: they must support *us*.'[27] The working class can be understood as a fractured collective constituted by a partly shared experience of exploitation and an antagonistic relationship to the wage relation which facilitates that exploitation. Not everyone is paid a wage, but everyone's life is impacted by the wage relation that deprives working-class people of what they need to live. Capital, the shared enemy, produces a fragmented universality and the call to unite behind those most harmed by the current distribution of work and resources. The movement sought to intervene in the field of revolutionary politics to institute a political subject dependent not on sameness but rather on differently located groups with a shared desire for an end to their exploitation.

Like the communist movement more broadly, the Wages for Housework campaign sought to produce demands that 'appear economically insufficient and untenable, but which, in the course of the movement, necessitate further inroads upon the old social order, and are unavoidable as a means of entirely revolutionising the mode of production'.[28] In the Wages for Housework articulation, the demands that would revolutionise the mode of (re)production were characteristically antiwork in nature. In her pamphlet 'Women, the Unions, and Work', James puts forward six demands for the movement, the first two of which are: '1. WE DEMAND TO WORK LESS ... 2. WE DEMAND A GUARANTEED INCOME FOR WOMEN AND FOR MEN, WORKING OR NOT WORKING, MARRIED OR NOT. WE DEMAND WAGES FOR HOUSEWORK.'[29] A Wages for Housework flyer from 1974 states:

Now we want to decide WHEN we work, HOW we work and WHO we work for. We want to be able to decide NOT TO WORK AT ALL ... Now we want back the wealth we have produced. WE WANT IT IN CASH, RETROACTIVE AND IMMEDIATELY. AND WE WANT ALL OF IT.[30]

The statement inverts the emotional blackmail that Wages for Housework writers contend is characteristic of women's condition under capitalism.[31] Instead, 'we' will take control of the exchange between labour and capital. This demand for the reclamation of wealth posits capital as the passive side of the class antagonism, merely supervising the work and capturing what workers produce. Through its demanding and immoderate tone, Wages for Housework seeks to constitute an autonomous feminist subject capable of collective emotional practices. Their work derives its power not necessarily from its political stringency but from its capacity to produce subjective states. The emotional charge of the demand, and its capacity for creating a collective feminist subject, are as central as its content.

According to the Wages for Housework authors, autonomy from male-dominated organisations on the left is essential for revolutionary feminism to create antagonistic practices that can develop the specific contradictions inherent in the sphere of reproduction.[32] This entailed women's self-organisation, as they are the workers most directly affected by such contradictions. As Wages for Housework members state in their collectively authored 'Theses on Wages for Housework': 'Autonomy from men is Autonomy from capital that uses men's power to discipline us.'[33] This practice sought to break with the emotional pressures of gendered relations – guilt and the internalised desire to be a good woman, responding to the authority of a man. Autonomy is not the same as separatism, as its goal is to develop solidarity with other movements and enough power to force the male-dominated left to concede to the demands and perspectives of revolutionary feminism. The purpose of autonomy is not to withdraw from organising with men but to find the demands on which such organisation would become possible – without erasing the specific exploitation of reproductive labour.

The point, then, is not to plead with men or enlighten them, but to show that autonomous organising outside of waged work is a source of power for the working class. As Federici succinctly states: 'Power educates. First men will fear, then they will learn because capital will fear.'[34] The naturalised emotional structures of gender, where women are taught to fear and respect the power of men, are inverted through a feminist project which builds autonomous power. Feminist autonomy therefore marks a break with the dominant order of emotional reproduction and creates space for new emotional practices. It is not through rational arguments that we will win men over to the feminist project but through building enough power to reverse hierarchy and structures of feeling.

Black and lesbian women formed autonomous groups within the Wages for Housework network, and sex workers organised autonomously in groups affiliated with Wages for Housework such as the English Collective of Prostitutes.[35] The idea of autonomy is most forcefully formulated by Brown. In her text 'The Autonomy of Black Lesbian Women', she argues that organising autonomously, and putting forward 'our particular vantage point of struggle', enables black lesbians to connect with other women without being marginalised as black women, made invisible, or assumed to be heterosexual.[36] For the women who often experience marginalisation within feminist movements, organising autonomously becomes a way of politicising forms of care that already happen in oppressed groups which have been forced to develop systems of emotional resilience and mutual care to compensate for the harms caused by oppression and exploitation. This is also a way of building powerful movements where care is a central part of the political project. Autonomy, then, is a source of strength for groups traditionally marginalised within left movements so that the entire working class can gain the power necessary to confront capitalism.

Wages for Refusal

Several Wages for Housework groups put out statements in solidarity with sex workers to respond to the increased repression they faced from the state. Wages for Housework interpreted this repression as another form of violent response to women's refusal of dependence and wagelessness. The San Francisco Wages for

Housework Committee states that 'although the government tries to isolate our struggles, we refuse to be divided. All work is prostitution and we are all prostitutes. We are forced to sell our bodies – for room and board or for cash – in marriage, in the street, in typing pools or in factories.'[37] This should be read in contrast to feminists who consider sex work an exceptional form of violence against women and thus separate sex workers from 'non-deviant' women.

Against the respectability politics of the anti-sex-work position, Wages for Housework authors read sex workers as being on the forefront of the struggle against sexual labour. Black Women for Wages for Housework draw connections between the policing of black women's supposedly excessive and deviant sexuality and the repression of sex workers.[38] Similarly, Wages Due Lesbians state that 'as lesbian women we, like prostitute women, refuse to accept that it is women's "nature" to sleep with men and to sleep with them "for love"'.[39] Wages for Housework understood lesbianism and paid sex work as ways to refuse doing the work of love for free. The lesbian refusal to sleep with men undermines men's power to command sexual labour. This does not mean that lesbianism is reducible to abstinence or refusal in the merely negative sense. Refusal is not a passive act of withdrawal of labour, but rather the construction of alternative ways of being. Lesbianism emerges as a refusal of the labour of love, as a way of moving away from a merely individualised notion of lesbian identity towards the idea of queerness as political practice. The Wages for Housework authors describe lesbian relationships as a form of resistance to the work ethic of heterosexuality. Heterosexuality, Wages Due Lesbians write, is the morality that says that all women 'naturally' serve men sexually and emotionally.[40]

As the group states in its 1975 founding document 'Fucking Is Work', the existence of lesbianism makes sex visible as labour, and a woman refusing this work is engaging in a partial refusal of her work as a woman.[41] Wages Due Lesbians member Ruth Hall argues that the rejection of heterosexuality is also a rejection of the notion that sexuality is a private matter.[42] Lesbianism thus has an explicitly political meaning when integrated into the overall Wages for Housework perspective. In the Wages Due Lesbians critique of heterosexuality, love is, as Weeks puts it, a way of desiring one's own unfreedom.[43] Refusing the narrow, institutionalised form of love opens a space for practices of resistance.

For the Wages for Housework authors, lesbianism has an important role as a political practice rather than as a given identity category. Lesbians occupy a pivotal position in the Wages for Housework struggle, as they are prefiguring the direction of the movement as a whole. Wages Due Lesbians presents lesbianism as 'an organizational form of women's struggle against work'.[44] In refusing part of the sexual and emotional labour that is assigned to most women, lesbians show that such resistance is possible – that there are other ways of being. Coming out as a lesbian, Federici states, is to go on strike.[45] While this refusal does not completely free lesbians of the labour of femininity, it does attack the structure of the family and its attendant work relations.[46]

Lesbian practices thus strike at the heart of gendered relations of labour. It is a rejection of the isolation of heterosexual institutions.[47] It is also a rejection of the narrowing of the sexual field, where romantic relationships with men are defined as fundamentally different from friendship with women. Federici writes:

> Early in our lives we must learn to draw a line between the people we can love and the people we just talk to, those to whom we can open our body and those to whom we can only open our 'souls', our lovers and our friends.

This demarcation is never fully sustainable since 'our bodies and emotions are indivisible and we communicate at all levels all the time'.[48] Lesbianism implies the work of beginning to undo some of these lines and the separate emotional spheres they impose. It also shows that these lines were never stable in the first place. Hall writes that capitalist conditions are contradictory in that the gendered division of labour encourages homosociality while excluding the potential for homosexuality and organises so-called leisure time heterosexually.[49] Lesbianism counters the restrictions on emotional and sexual practice imposed by the heterosexual work ethic.

However, Wages Due Lesbians also described the forms of violence and labour that lesbianism entails. Because lesbian relationships are made invisible by the societal celebration of (heterosexual, romantic) love, and lesbians are frequently subjected to physical and emotional violence, lesbianism entails its own form of emotional reproduction. The very refusal that lesbians stage when they reject the labour of loving men also makes lesbians more likely to be marked as targets for disciplinary violence. This violence in turn increases the need for a different kind of emotional reproduction. Hall argues that lesbianism can bring more work because 'there's so much pressure all the time on all of us that we are continually having to struggle to hold each other together and keep sane'.[50] This emotional pressure, however, might point to the uses of negative emotions in creating and sustaining counter-hegemonic forms of collective subjectivity. Heather Love writes that 'modern homosexual identity is formed out of and in relation to the experience of social damage'.[51] The experiences that Hall describes can tell us something about how damage can lead to the creation of new and collective forms of care.

Lesbianism, while containing some utopian elements, is not in itself a revolutionary form of sociality because it still exists within a structurally violent system of capitalist reproduction. Opting out of this system is not an individual choice. Wages Due Lesbians authors rejected the idea that moving to a separatist lesbian commune could solve the contradictions of reproductive labour.[52] Against a strategy of withdrawal and separatism, Wages Due Lesbians practised solidarity with heterosexual women based on partially shared material conditions. The autonomous structure of Wages Due Lesbians made sure that lesbian concerns would be heard in Wages for Housework activism, and Wages Due Lesbians members were aware that solidarity could not come at the cost of ignoring difference under the generic label of 'women'. However, they did pay careful attention to the ways in which lesbian women are not freed from being interpellated by feminised labour. To the extent that lesbians are called upon to perform various forms of reproductive work, they are still within the devalued social category of women. This is because reproduction is not confined to the heterosexual relationship but stretches across a range of different social relations, including waged work. While lesbians are denied the label of 'real women' because of their rejection of the intimate labours of heterosexual romantic love, they are nonetheless captive in a broader logic of gendered reproduction.[53]

For the Wages for Housework writers, the most important limitation of lesbian separatism is that lesbianism does not exist outside of the capitalist organisation of the reproductive sphere. It is not enough to make the individual decision to not take part in relationships with men. As long as heterosexual formations dominate the social totality, lesbian relationships are likely to reproduce at least some of the structures of reproductive work that operate in heterosexual families. As Federici puts it, 'Homosexuality is workers' control of production, not the end of work.'[54] Lesbianism is a form of immanent resistance, as lesbian identity was made possible by the creation of heterosexuality. Therefore it enables a political subjectivity that can challenge heterosexual, capitalist reproduction, but lesbianism in itself is not a solution to the contradictions of capitalist reproduction or the exploitation of reproductive labour. It is a way of moving through the subjectivities produced by the capitalist organisation of labour and hopefully coming out on the other side. Only the end of capitalist production and reproduction could fundamentally change the current organisation of the heterosexual nuclear family, the household, and the gender division of labour, and vice versa; only the abolition of the family could spell the end of capitalism.

Wages for Housework did not advocate for political lesbianism in the same way that many radical feminists did. Federici writes that the movement cannot impose a new model for sexuality when the goal of the movement is self-determination.[55] In the Wages for Housework literature, there is also a sense that relationships with men could be different if social relations were different. Men are only the enemy insofar as they have been assigned a role of control over women. The deeper problem is a gendered division of labour that sets men and women against each other. Heterosexual relationships would have to be radically reconstituted through the subversion of that division of labour, which according to the Wages for Housework authors would require the overturning of the capitalist system as we know it. But Wages for Housework writers do not think heterosexuality can be fixed just by changing the division of labour within the household. This is especially true since so much of gender as we know it is organised around heterosexual arrangements, and it would be misleading to even speak of heterosexuality if those formations of gender were drastically subverted.

Wages Due Lesbians argued that we do not know how many women are (or could be) lesbians, because lesbianism has not yet become a viable choice for many women. The group supported a wage for housework on the basis that it would give women, both lesbian and (currently) heterosexual, more time and freedom, and more options to build emotional and sexual relationships differently.[56] As Wages Due Lesbians Toronto members state, 'Wages for housework means wages against heterosexuality.'[57] The demand for wages for housework is not only a way of refusing some of the labour of femininity but also a tool for undermining heterosexual institutions.

The demand for a wage for housework was thus never intended as a reformist demand for redistribution of resources within existing social relations. Federici contests the argument that a bit of money would not make much of a difference, arguing that we could never get that money 'without at the same time revolutionizing – in the process of struggling for it – all our family and social relations'.[58] This is especially true of currently unwaged emotional labour, whose meaning changes in the process of becoming waged work. As we have seen, however, the unmeasurable quality of emotional labour places limits on its commodification. The political potential of wages for housework as a demand is also its unreasonableness – it would be impossible to adequately remunerate all currently unwaged and low-waged work. Waged work in capitalism depends on the unwaged work of producing sociality and wellbeing, making total commodification impossible. The demand for wages for housework, and in particular for the totality of emotional labour to be remunerated, is unrealisable under the current order of things. Far from being a reformist demand for an allowance, wages for housework as a political demand becomes a tool for pointing to the structural exclusions in the production of value. It is an immoderate demand for the totality of that immeasurable work to be remunerated retroactively. Wages for Housework rejected the myth of liberation through work. The demand for wages for housework was meant to allow women to say, 'We have worked enough.'[59]

The usefulness of the demand for a wage cannot be determined theoretically, but as Dalla Costa points out, it is effective as a demand to the extent that it produces the 'strength and confidence' necessary to constitute a collective feminist subject.[60] The construction of political demands and movements, then, cannot happen solely through disembodied intellectual labour, but must include the production of emotional and collective counter-hegemonic subjectivities. It is through coalitions of bad mothers, sex workers, queers, and other deviant reproductive subjects that we can begin to make another world.

By locating the struggle in the sphere of the home and the community, the members of Wages for Housework sought to highlight that rather than being a non-political and non-productive domain, political struggle over reproduction could cause significant disruption to the capitalist circuit. While Wages for Housework never became a mass movement, and never accomplished the aim of fully refusing reproductive labour, its members understood the potential of an antiwork struggle on the site of reproduction. As Dalla Costa contends, *'No strike has ever been a general strike'* – as long as unwaged work is not recognised and refused, we have not used all the means of disruption available to us.[61] The political potential of a coordinated refusal of work is as yet unexplored. But a nascent wave of feminist organising is using the name of the strike to invoke the refusal of reproductive work – a refusal which is simultaneously impossible and necessary.[62]

The demand for wages for housework cannot be understood divorced from its context – that is, the attempt to constitute an antagonistic feminist subject capable of refusal. As we have seen, this also depends on a politics of emotion in which anger and the emotional practice of solidarity constitute modes of refusal essential for the struggle for a different world. These emotional practices involve both recuperating bad feelings and unlearning habitual and constraining emotional responses. The Wages for Housework project depends on repurposing outlaw emotions to broaden the horizon of possible emotional practices. Emotion becomes communal. It is understood no longer as the inner truth of an individual, but as a collective habit that can become a political tool. As Weeks points out, the feminist collective is also a desiring subject.[63] It wants more than what is offered. It refuses to be content with reforming the site of reproduction and refuses the call for men to 'help' with domestic labour. These calls leave the social relations of domestic work intact, which explains why women have continued to bear the primary responsibility for reproduction. Wages for Housework wanted to bring into being a collective feminist subject with the capacity to make demands for a different world. What does this subject want? The abolition of feminised labour and its attendant work relations.

5

A Different Feeling

Feminism is often articulated as a movement for gender equality. But in a socio-economic system fundamentally based on restricted access to material and social resources and differentiating divisions of labour, the equality discourse will always be limited. Equality is a bourgeois political concept which relies on the erasure of substantial differences between different material conditions.[1] This is not to say that the concept of equality can never be mobilised in a radical way. In the course of feminist history, the term has been used to give women access to previously masculine spheres and a degree of independence from men. But today, many women are exploited in both waged and unwaged forms of labour. Precisely because equality is a core term in the liberal political imagination, it can be useful as well as limited. It can be used to increase the legal rights of different marginalised groups. But the discourse of equality has taken us to a limit-point in feminist politics, and it must now be replaced with a move towards the abolition of feminised labour, the family, and gender.

The politics of equality has mainly resulted in women's increased access to waged work, and indeed the increased compulsion to participate in the labour force. For working-class women, equality with exploited male workers is not a very attractive political vision. Unlike most liberal feminists, who encouraged women to leave the home to pursue a career, some Marxist feminist thinkers of the 1970s predicted that a majority of women would be performing repetitive and low-waged forms of work once they became part of the formal labour force. Coming from an antiwork perspective, the

Wages for Housework theorists argue that more work is a way of increasing women's subordination.[2] And doing waged work has not enabled women to refuse most unwaged work. While standards for unwaged work can be reduced, this work cannot be completely abandoned, as most people could not pay for all the reproductive services they need. Waged work is therefore performed on top of women's unwaged work. This double burden leaves less time for resisting exploitation. While Wages for Housework feminists sought to refuse unwaged work, their aim was not for women to have equal access to career paths or having to work another job outside the home. Rather they demanded more time for themselves, and time to join other women in struggle.

Wages for Housework drew inspiration from the work of the National Welfare Rights Organization, a group consisting mainly of black mothers who received benefits. These women refused waged work on the basis that they were already working as mothers. Their labour as mothers was devalued because black women were primarily valued as waged workers reproducing white families.[3] Sara Farris has shown that in contemporary Europe, the labour of immigrant women of colour is devalued in a similar way, thus forcing these women to perform low-waged care work for others, often the same work that bourgeois white women have been able to refuse to do for free.[4]

Wages for Housework authors frequently criticised leftist organisations that suggested that housewives and other unwaged people should join the working class by becoming part of the industrial proletariat, arguing that housewives were already working.[5] In this way, the Wages for Housework strategy is articulated against both liberal feminism, with its aim of allowing some (white, bourgeois) women to become the bearers of power under capitalism, and the socialist strategy that suggested that class struggle can only be carried out by waged workers on the terrain of capitalist production. The continued relevance of the legacy of the welfare-rights movement and Wages for Housework is that these movements offered a different perspective from the mainstream feminist movement, which demanded the emancipation of women through labour-force participation and equal rights. We cannot leave unwaged workers behind by suggesting that there is a moral or political value in waged work. Wages for Housework writers argue that career opportunities could never lead to liberation, as such 'solutions' to women's status as unwaged labour depend on someone else doing reproductive labour.[6] These individualised solutions tend to create a racist hierarchy between 'modern', career-oriented white women and supposedly backwards migrant women doing reproductive work.[7]

The reorganisation of gender relations in the neoliberal era has deepened the divisions between women who are at least partially able to live up to the ideals of masculine subjectivity and those who are stuck with traditionally feminised labour. The feminist politics of equality has allowed some (mostly white) women to gain more power while obscuring the increasing inequality between women. Both liberal and socialist feminists have often failed to find a solution to these divisions. For liberal feminists, the main concern is sexist discrimination within the waged workplace, with little examination of how waged work itself is built on a system of unwaged work. For some socialist feminists, the emphasis has been on making sure that women could join men in performing productive work, and thus join the working-class struggle against exploitation. This is a long-running theme in socialist and Marxist writings on 'the woman question', going back to Engels's 1884 book *The Origin of the Family, Private Property and the State*.[8] The focus on women's entrance into wage labour entailed a struggle for state services that would allow women to work outside their homes, most importantly childcare provision. These services have historically played the role of supplementing the family as the sphere of reproductive work while allowing more women to become part of a low-waged proletariat.[9]

Just as social-democratic states have often worked to save capitalism from its own worst excesses, the feminist politics of the welfare state serve to protect the nuclear family from some of the contradictions that are inherent in this social form. In particular, it has sought to address the fact that while the family is supposedly the site where our needs are met, families have never been able to do all of this work or meet the needs of all people. Welfare-state feminism has worked to save the family from itself and its own logic of violence and exploitation. This form of feminism has always been heteronormative and white. It has taken a particular form of the family for granted while seeking to minimise the damage and hierarchy produced by it. Needless to say, these attempts have mostly been in vain.

Given that capitalism relies on hierarchical divisions of labour and splits within the workforce, it has often not meant increased equal opportunity. In fact, it has often worked in the opposite direction. What Silvia Federici calls 'the myth of capitalism as the great equalizer' cannot account for the contradictory organisation of capitalist reproduction and the continuing stratification of the labour market.[10] While equality feminisms have sought to universalise men's working conditions, such a political horizon is both undesirable and impossible given the continued reliance on unwaged and low-waged reproductive work. Neoliberal political discourse often uses a gender-neutral language of equal access. But its invocations of 'individual responsibility' and 'community care' in fact depend on the reproduction of more or less normative family relationships and women's continued responsibility for unwaged reproductive labour. This is because liberal individualism simultaneously disavows and depends on the existence of reproductive labour, and emotional reproduction in particular.

While women have gained increased access to waged work, somewhat more equal opportunities within the formal economy have not necessarily translated into a reorganisation of the division of labour in the household. The model of a male bread-winner and a female homemaker has been superseded in the sphere of waged work, but assumptions relating to the provision of informal care have not necessarily changed.[11] This means that the overarching responsibility for care still falls dispropor-tionately on women. The paradigm of equality within main-stream feminism has translated into a double burden for women, exacerbated by increased precarity in the sphere of production and the decimation of state services within the sphere of reproduction.

Within the sphere of unwaged reproductive labour, equality politics tend to be limited and individualising. Because this aspect of life has been marked as private in capitalist econo-mies, individual choice reigns as a hegemonic political discourse. Equality discourse in the domestic sphere has been focused on getting men to do their fair share, rather than a rethinking of the domestic as such. Selma James writes that the male-dominated reformist left is unable to think beyond the current organisation of the domestic sphere: 'They can as little conceive of destroying the institution of the family as they can of the factory.'[12] The mainstream left's emphasis on productivity and 'good jobs' is connected to its attachments to normative family values, demanding nothing more than a 'fair wage' which can be used to buy a house and start a family. The bourgeois good life is reframed as an aspiration for the working class, retaining its normative and reactionary content. In the same way, equality politics tend to accept the domestic sphere as a given reality, merely reshuffling some of the work within this sphere, rather than trying to break down the divi-sions that separate domestic and waged work as such.

Much of mainstream feminism has encouraged men to get involved in reproductive labour, in particular childcare. Part of women's struggle against reproductive work is also to force men to assume responsibility for this work. But teaching men to do reproductive labour, without challenging the conflicting needs and contradictions within capitalism, will only take us so far. Federici writes that 'trying to educate men has always meant that our struggle was privatized and fought in the solitude of our kitchens and bedrooms'.[13] A problem with these strategies, then, is that they often appear as merely individual. Constituting reproductive struggles must also be a project of collectivising reproduction.

The idea that men should help out at home does little to rearticulate the labour relations and relations of power that instituted the domestic in the first place. It does not address the fact that women tend to retain the overarching responsibility for making sure that domestic work gets done, even when the tasks of domestic work are shared more equally. As we have seen, domestic labour cannot be reduced to a set of chores, but rather implies a relation of labour exploitation. Equality politics has been less able to address this relation, thus leaving the mental and emotional labour of the domestic sphere untouched. These more invisible forms of labour tend to remain unequally distributed even in supposedly egalitarian relationships.[14] Owing to the link between the family form and the organisation of the waged economy, intimate notions of difference and broader social hierarchies continue to be reproduced.

A politics of equality cannot address the hierarchical structure built into the very notion of gender. Gender equality, as a conceptual framework, operates within the paradigm of sexual difference. The term equality cannot help but invoke the notion of difference, since it implies an equality between different parties which supposedly pre-exists inequality and will continue to exist in the absence of oppression. While erasing social difference – the real conditions under which people live – the concept of equality also presumes an eternal and pre-social form of sexual difference. Sexual difference already contains a construction of hierarchy, making 'gender equality'

a contradiction in terms. Because it is built around an understanding of this equality as operating within the heterosexual
couple, whose very relation is based on subordination, gender
equality cannot be realised within its own terms. Equality
politics, then, especially in the sphere of the domestic, remains
a type of heterosexual reformism – hoping that heterosexual
relationships could become better while leaving the institution
of the family intact.[15]

Patricia Cain argues that equality discourse continues to
privilege masculinity as the standard against which women's
sameness or difference is measured.[16] This means that heterosexual masculinity, which is produced through difference
from femininity, implicitly becomes the (impossible) standard
for femininity. Femininity, then, is what needs to be erased in
a politics of equality, as some women are encouraged to adopt
the subject position of possessive individualism in order to
enter the workforce on the same terms as men. But as we saw
in chapter 3, this leads to contradictory demands even for
those relatively privileged women who are able to precariously inhabit possessive individualism. Because of the supposedly independent subjectivity's hidden reliance on its opposite,
the dependent reproductive labourer, femininity cannot be
fully erased. Equality politics create a punitive and contradictory situation, even for white bourgeois women – the erasure
of femininity is a precondition for their success in the sphere
of waged work, while they are simultaneously punished if
they become too masculine. Although gender equality has
been realised in some limited and formal senses, this has often
served to reproduce gender relations in less apparent and visible ways.

Johanna Oksala suggests that only the full commodification
of currently unwaged work could lead to equality under capitalism, as women's unwaged obligations mark them as less
valuable as labouring subjects. However, she also stresses that
the intimacy of emotional labour and the work of pregnancy

make it impossible to commodify those relations without drastically changing their meaning.[17] It would therefore be impossible to reach full equality while retaining the nuclear family form as the privileged reproductive arrangement.

But this does not mean that a better feminist politics should consist in valuing femininity on its own terms, as some feminists have argued. This sometimes takes the form of the demand that women's unwaged work should be counted or estimations of the contributions of care work to the nation's GDP.[18] However, there are limits to merely counting and valorising feminised work. Mariarosa Dalla Costa writes that such counting might contribute to the 'draining and dispersal of women's energies in the long run, and with respect to a goal of dubious value'.[19] It is also unclear how a feminist valorisation of this work could come about. Part of the reason that reproductive work, and particularly white bourgeois motherhood, is morally glorified is that it lacks monetary rewards. The declaration that this unwaged work should be made visible and valorised does not change the material arrangements that currently serve to devalorise it.

Moreover, even if women's large-scale entry into the sphere of waged work had resulted in a genuine redistribution of labour in the home, it would not necessarily solve other issues around reproduction under capitalism. Reproductive work would still have punitive effects for those inside and outside of normative family arrangements. As Cameron Lynne Macdonald argues, increased paternal participation in childcare is at most a partial solution, since it is based on the idea of the nuclear family as an isolated unit with its own limited resources.[20] Men's increased participation in domestic labour and childcare would not provide a solution to the constricted time and resources allocated for reproduction under capitalism. While state-provided services could mitigate this issue to some extent, they tend to be patchwork and focused on enabling mothers to participate in waged work while raising children. State-provided services are also often inaccessible to those who do not live up to certain conditions. They therefore function to discipline families, particularly mothers.[21] For example, benefits recipients often have to behave in a certain way, and perform 'good' standards of reproduction, in order not to lose what little monetary support they get.

The implication that the family should be the primary source of care does not address the uneven distribution of emotional labour for those who are, for various reasons, excluded from the family. Nor does a politics that promotes equality within the domestic sphere account for the fact that the family is a privileged site of care because it structurally excludes those who are not participating in normative family arrangements. Rather than campaigning for men's increased participation in domestic work, and state services to compensate when parental work is not enough, we should strive for the abolition of the family and its attendant relations of gender and labour. A successful reproductive revolution would have to intervene within the domestic sphere in order to undo the separation between the private and the public.

Abolishing the Family

In order to get out of the bind of equality, which continues to rely on fundamentally hierarchical, exploitative, and exclusionary social relations, we need to move towards abolishing the family. Family abolition is not merely about breaking down existing forms of kinship and work relationships. Instead, what we need is a positive form of abolition, capable of producing a viable alternative to the status quo; in other words, negation and affirmation together. Abolition is closely linked to the political strategy of refusal of work, in that the aim of the negative strategy is not merely destructive but rather provides the imaginary for something new.

When thinking about the abolition of gender and the family, we can draw on other abolitionist traditions, such as the movement to abolish slavery and the current struggle to abolish prisons. Liat Ben-Moshe, citing W. E. B. Du Bois, argues that the abolition of slavery failed to end racial oppression because it was a merely negative reform, and suggests that prison abolition must have a positive programme.[22] For Fred Moten and Stefano Harney, prison abolition is 'not so much the abolition of prisons but the abolition of a society that could have prisons'.[23] This means that in order to fully undo the punitive and violent social logic of prisons, we must find other ways of being together which can address the root causes of violence. Similarly, the abolition of family and gender must contend with the logics that continually reproduce gendered hierarchies, exploitative forms of kinship, and the very need for families. We cannot abolish gender or the family simply by ignoring them. Rather, we must address and disrupt the underlying causes and contradictions of gendered reproduction.

Abolition means the end of the repetition of sameness. Sara Ahmed writes that heterosexuality, based on notions of gendered difference, is bound up with the desire to reproduce the same. The heterosexual bond 'gets structured around the desire to "reproduce well". Good reproduction is often premised around a fantasy of "making likeness".'[24] After all, what is the good life apart from the repetition of the same – those who already have access to comfort ensuring its continuation? Heterosexual reproduction seems future-oriented in its emphasis on creating a good life for one's children. But this future looks exactly the same as the present. Abolition can be understood as the proliferation of difference, both in terms of the proliferation of a multitude of subject positions and in terms of a break from the present.[25] This is not the naturalised and binary sexual difference assumed by equality feminism, but a genuine difference that challenges the erasures of social difference that the concept of equality performs. As such, it involves the conscious failure to reproduce as labour power in terms of its subjective orientation towards docility and discipline. It also involves the failure to engage with the work ethic of heterosexuality. A queer communism must challenge the organisation of both waged and unwaged work.

It is important to note that in seeking to abolish the family and gender, the target of this perspective is nuclear families and white, binary heterogender. These social forms are hegemonic – they dominate all of society. Yet they impact various groups of people in different ways. The present is not a coherent totality but contains elements that can be mobilised for a different future. Black feminists, including Wilmette Brown, Angela Davis, Hazel Carby, Hortense Spillers, and bell hooks, have long argued that black kinship has a different political meaning than white nuclear families, and is less dependent on female subordination.[26] However, hooks suggests that black families have become increasingly invested in white bourgeois family ideals in ways that undo some of the radical potential of black kinship.[27] Similarly, several scholars have pointed to the normative ideals that structure many gay and lesbian couples and families.[28] We cannot take for granted the antinormative or subversive character of marginalised people's reproductive lives. Some people within marginalised groups can be at least partially and precariously integrated into the logic of family values. This may in fact strengthen such values by making them appear more tolerant and flexible. We should, however, pay attention to how many arrangements existing in the present are already marked as deviant. These devalued kinship structures can contain at least the inspiration for a radical practice on the terrain of reproduction.

The political framework of family abolition has become increasingly well known over the past few years, but it is not a new position. The perspective has a long history in the communist tradition, and can be traced back to *The Communist Manifesto*. For Marx and Engels, the call to abolish the family stems from their rejection of the bourgeois family form, which is bound up with private property and men's claim to ownership over their wives.[29] Families are more than carriers of normative values. Families are work relations, and in particular a central site of emotional reproduction. The family is a privatised arrangement of work, care, and economic distribution, shored up by ideological and legal means. Furthermore, families function to structure kinship and lines of inheritance, or lack thereof – forms of (dis)possession that are tied to the reproduction of classed and racial difference. Sophie Lewis writes that ' "family" refers to "blood" ideology and organized care scarcity: a kind of anti-queerness machine for shoring up race/class and producing binary-gendered workers'.[30] The family is tied up with the production of gender, the exclusion of queerness, and the continued reproduction of overlapping racial and classed dynamics. Family abolition is a necessary part of the abolition of private property.

In a similar vein, Jules Joanne Gleeson and Kade Doyle Griffiths argue that since the family is an economic unit, critiquing the patriarchal or heteronormative values of family relationships is insufficient. They write that 'not many will accept their children losing social advantages which they possess. The absence of alternative institutions of obligation ensures that this is felt as a binding burden: beyond the family, there are merely individuals.'[31] The challenge of the abolitionist project is to think of how the work that families do can be transformed and diffused rather than just abandoned, and how we can create other forms of bonds so that we can be more than 'merely individuals'. We cannot replace family units with detached individuals, as individuals, both adults and children, cannot meet many of their own needs. In Gleeson and Griffiths's words, 'A purely negative effort to destroy the family would simply result in starving infants', and, I would add, many lonely and sick adults.[32]

Contrary to some articulations of family abolition, I argue that it cannot just mean the expansion of existing kinship models. Because the family is a fundamentally exclusionary social form, and one based on a zero-sum model of emotional bonds, we cannot just expect to abolish the family by including more people in our intimate sphere while leaving existing family relationships intact. Family abolition does not mean inviting more people over for family dinner. Because current and dominant models of kinship are based on scarcity and property, family abolition means that how we relate to our biological kin would change fundamentally, to the point where these relations would no longer be recognisable to us. They would become less emotionally charged and fraught.

The demand for family abolition must be articulated according to the specific form the family has taken in different historical phases. Whereas for Marx and Engels, 'the family' meant the emerging hegemony of bourgeois family values, the feminist writings of the sixties and seventies target the twentieth-century male-breadwinner model of a working-class family. As M. E. O'Brien shows, this family model was won through extensive working-class struggle, and therefore family abolitionists had to position themselves against the grain of the mainstream workers' movement.[33] Shifting models of (re)production have further unravelled the already limited access to the kinds of protection and emotional security that the mid-century white nuclear family model offered.

Today, a heightened dependence on commodified reproductive services indicates that the family has become increasingly precarious – something that parts of the left consider a worrying sign of neoliberalism's impact on communities and human relationality.[34] Arlie Russell Hochschild's later writings, for example, articulate a socialist position that defends an expanded notion of the family, which now includes single parents and homosexual couples raising children.[35] This new and inclusive notion of family, the argument goes, must be protected against the neoliberal commodification of human relationships. According to this logic, the family is under threat, and we need to find solutions that would protect family life. But as Sarah Brouillette points out, 'The family has not been destroyed enough.'[36] A socialist politics that seeks to defend the family against the onslaught of neoliberal individualism has missed the fact that family values and familial labour are in fact essential conditions for the existence of such individualism.

What can account for the persistence of nuclear family models after the end of the family wage and the breadwinner model? One reason the family remains a hegemonic form, even as it has become more precarious and flexible than it was in the post-war period, is that we have failed to construct viable alternatives. The nuclear family appears increasingly unstable, as indicated by higher divorce rates and seemingly more inclusive norms surrounding family arrangements. This has led to a discourse of the family being in crisis. But no new model has taken its place, and access to care and resources often remains tied to membership in a family. People keep imagining familial relations as the source of the good life, despite how inadequate they are in terms of meeting the emotional and physical needs of most people.

In undoing the privatisation of family, we must also abolish the privatisation of feeling. The family under capitalism functions as a nexus of privatised emotional bonds. Emotional labour has to be refused for a feminist movement to be able to mobilise emotion in an emancipatory way. This refusal means doing emotion differently. I am not arguing against emotional care for other people. Rather, I want to articulate a politics in which we struggle against emotional reproduction as we know it – that is, tied up with forms of sociality and ideology that continually recreate and privilege privatised social bonds and hierarchically constituted subjectivities. Abolishing the family and gender involves the ungendering of emotion. It also involves moving away from niceness as the dominant good feeling, and accepting or even cultivating bad feeling. As a dominant family value of the bourgeoisie, niceness has a tendency to obscure social hierarchy, exploitation, and antagonisms. Niceness has a propensity to travel upwards in the social hierarchy, accumulating at the top and associating those at the bottom with bad feeling and emotional stigma. In order to abolish emotional labour and bourgeois family values, niceness has to be deprivileged as a socially desirable feeling. This might mean that we all have to live with some emotional discomfort, rather than allowing comfort to adhere to the most privileged. It would mean refusing the good life as we know it – a life of good jobs, home ownership, and proprietarian family relationships.

The family is intimately tied up with structures of class, race, and heterosexuality through naturalised notions of genetics and bloodlines. It is also entangled with capitalist property relations through practices of inheritance and the privatisation of kinship, as well as the imaginary of family as a form of ownership of other people. Family abolition must thus be the abolition of naturalised, proprietarian forms of kinship and labour.[37] The social relations that could support non-hierarchical, reciprocal, and non-proprietarian modes of kinship cannot be realised under capitalism. Therefore, the movement to abolish the family must be concomitant with movements to abolish capital as well as other structures of dominance such as race and heterosexuality.

It is important to remember the compensatory function of emotional reproduction – it is often the work that makes up for unsatisfactory conditions and creates niceness where, for most people, there is none. The movement to abolish emotional reproduction can only happen in conjunction with the struggle for conditions that do not deplete us emotionally. Emotional reproduction, then, cannot be resisted on its own but has to be put in the context of the conditions that create the need for it. The abolition of emotional reproduction is in turn a necessary condition for abolishing the gendered and racialised subjectivities to which it gives rise. In refusing the good life, we are struggling for something else. This something would be better for a majority of people, since it would resist the punitive and harmful effects of the good life on those aspiring to it as well as those who are excluded from it. It would be a new way of relating emotionally to one another. 'Will that association be a family?' James asks, and continues: 'It can only be so different from what humanity has known before that we may find a new name for it.'[38]

Gender Abolition

In abolishing the family and feminised forms of labour, the feminist movement must also strive to abolish gender itself. This involves a project of denaturalising gender and moving towards a form of subjectivity where assigned gender is increasingly felt as an 'external constraint' rather than the inner truth of the subject.[39] But a merely negative effort to abolish gender, without addressing its economic structure in the family and reproductive labour, would be very limited. Simply rejecting existing categories only amounts to the relinquishing of important conceptual tools for feminist theorising and activism. This prematurely decrees the end of gender, rather than moving through identity by using it as an organising tool.

By contrast, Maya Gonzalez's influential text 'Communization and the Abolition of Gender' links abolition to the movement of communism. Here, communism as 'the real movement which abolishes the present state of things' also involves the abolition of gender as one of the central antagonisms that structure the present.[40] However, Gonzalez reads gender abolition primarily in the context of capitalist population control, and therefore in relation to pregnancy.[41] From Gonzalez's account, it is difficult to say how gender will be abolished other than through the invention of extra-uterine biological reproduction. But gender abolition cannot be reduced to the undoing of pregnancy, as gender cannot be reduced to the difference of the pregnant body. As we have seen, gendering involves the construction of certain subjects as caring and intersubjective, whereas others are marked as essentially independent of social constraints and needs.

Both of these versions of gender abolition fail to articulate a sufficiently expansive notion of gender linking it to a range of social relations. For Shulamith Firestone, the abolition of gender can only occur through the radical restructuring of households and models of kinship. This is arguably more important for her than technological interventions into pregnancy, despite her reputation as a techno-utopian.[42] With Firestone, we can try to think about the necessary conditions for the remaking of gender through the material conditions of reproduction. If femininity is a work function, the abolition of gender is necessarily part and parcel of a feminist antiwork and antifamily position. The abolition of gender is thus tightly intertwined with family abolition. As James suggests, the radical rethinking of reproductive work and gender arrangements would lead to the end of the family as we know it. She writes that 'it is not only the division of labor between men and women which must be altered but the nature of that labor itself'.[43] This, she suggests, would spell 'the end of bourgeois society and of the bourgeois family with it'.[44]

Going beyond radically changing the conditions and relations of labour that currently structure reproduction, gender abolition would involve undoing all the restrictions of gender identity and stripping bodily markers of their social significance.[45] This means following black, indigenous, trans, and intersex feminists, who have long struggled against the physical and psychic imposition of binary, white heterogender. The fact that reproduction is also the reproduction of white families and nations allows us to think about how gender and race are co-constitutive. Trans feminism also challenges naturalised conceptions of gender and family. Reading trans femininity not as an affirmation of womanhood but as its partial destruction, Gleeson situates trans feminism as a movement against womanhood. The inclusion of trans women in the naturalised category of womanhood threatens the very coherence of that category.[46] A trans feminist project of abolition should be understood as more than either a merely nihilist or negative undoing of gender, or a simple affirmation of pre-existing models of gendered subjectivity. It involves a more complicated project of gender abolition in which binary gendered subjectivity is undermined through the denaturalising choice of a gendered life other than that which is socially imposed. This does not imply that all trans people are committed to abolishing gender, but rather that trans feminist perspectives are essential for an abolitionist project that refuses to take biological sex as the underlying truth of gender. As Maya Gonzalez and Jeanne Neton argue, sex and gender are two sides of the same coin and can only be abolished together.[47]

Transphobic feminists often suggest that trans people reinforce stereotypical gender presentations. Through this argument, they position themselves as the true gender abolitionists. But in this effort, they come to police gender and sex, and insist that our gender presentation should be consistent with our assigned sex. Transphobic feminism in fact undermines gender abolition. Like the lesbian forms of resistance explored in chapter 4, trans movements can be understood as an immanent form of resistance against the imposition of gender. This means that trans identity is not an expression of a more authentic form of subjectivity but instead an unexpected product of the same system that imposes cis gender identities. This outlawed form of subjectivity offers a point from which to resist the imposition of gender identity as such. It is a way of resisting by *moving through* gender in order to move towards a world in which cis and trans become meaningless terms because gender/sex have been abolished and masculine and feminine forms of gender presentation are available to everyone without stigmatisation.

Gender identities are never fully coherent and stable. But as we have seen, the contradictions they give rise to can in many cases be incorporated into binary constructions of gender. Contemporary models of gender in particular seem to allow for a degree of flexibility. A gender abolitionist project must therefore seek to highlight and heighten the contradictions of gender, pointing to its inherent instability and challenging the process of renaturalising gender. In this way, gender could be experienced less as an inner truth of the self, internalised in part through the performance of emotional labour. Instead, it could come to be experienced as a management technique and an external imposition.

The abolition of gender is impossible without the abolition of heterosexuality and sexual identities more broadly. This might entail giving up some of the pleasures that people currently experience as part of heterosexual gender performance. Queer thought and practice, however, gesture towards the possibility of other pleasures, currently made unthinkable by the imposition of sexual identity as an inner truth. For James, the gay movement opens the way for an individuality free of sexual identity.[48] James describes queer politics, the lesbian movement in particular, as being on the forefront of the struggle against current gender relations. This is similar to Kevin Floyd's queer Marxism, in which both heterosexuality and homosexuality are described as reified social categories. For Floyd, like James, we must move through these identity categories in order to go beyond them.[49] James links this to a feminist project in which the abolition of sexual identity is tied to a refusal of normative reproductive relationships. As gay and lesbian identities emerged through their exclusion from the heterosexual family, these forms can be productively used in a struggle that ultimately points beyond sexual identity as such. Queer feminism is therefore essential for the positive abolition of gender through the invention of new gendered and sexual ways of being.

Abolition involves the undoing of privileged forms of subjectivity and reproduction, which have real and violent effects on all of us – especially those who fail to live up to these forms, or refuse to aspire to them. Such excluded forms of reproduction can tell us something about alternative forms of life and how to build a different future. This requires not only the rejection of binary gender norms and nuclear family structures but radical intervention into the lived forms of reproduction in which people engage. This cannot be a politics that merely aims to expand the privileges of the family to include less normative family constellations, as such privileges are the result of the exclusions on which the family form depends. Instead, it has to challenge the very form of the family, and seek to create other reproductive arrangements and horizons of feeling.

Queering Emotional Reproduction

Starting from the position that our current organisation of social life cannot adequately meet the needs and desires of most people, we might look at some forms of sociality that move away from individualism, privacy, and property. Kathi Weeks argues that we should not pretend to know too much too soon, or seek a ready-made blueprint for future sociality.[50] But as Firestone remarks, we might still need to make utopian gestures towards the future, in order to counter 'the peculiar failure of imagination' concerning alternatives to the family'.[51] We have to work out these possibilities in practice rather than just conceptually. Such work is often difficult, as we struggle against material restrictions and to unlearn habitual emotional responses, but it is a crucial aspect of moving towards a more liveable world.

I use the concept of queering to highlight how currently deviant practices of reproduction can be mobilised to undo some of the institutionalised modes of reproduction that structure the present. Queerness is on the side of a different future because heterosexuality is so tightly imbricated with social and material forms of property – that is, with the preservation of sameness. New forms of sociality will require the innovative reorganisation of material resources and practices that 'can create and sustain alternative values, needs, and desires'.[52] These are modes of queer world-making in which counter-hegemonic practices of sociality can be formed.

Such practices are not the only or even the most important form of politics. Alternative practices of care cannot fully prefigure the new forms of gendered and sexual relations that we want.[53] The material constraints that these alternative practices come up against shows that alternative forms of sociality are structurally limited. This means that we need to engage in efforts to break down the boundaries of production and reproduction, and struggle across currently divided spheres. Rather than prefiguring a different world or offering a ready-made alternative to the existing mode of production, non-normative forms of reproduction offer sites from which to struggle. These attempts at queer world-making, always limited in their scope, can illustrate 'that this world is not enough'.[54] Like outlaw emotions, then, experiments in alternative forms of reproduction can provide epistemological tools for an anti-capitalist politics while also providing some of the material and emotional support we need to continue the struggle. A politics based on queer reproduction will constantly come upon constraints where capitalist forms of work, property, and sociality block alternative modes of being. But these limits are in themselves important – by identifying them, we can find ways to struggle against them. Queer reproduction is an expansive project that seems to remake not just the domestic sphere but the world as we know it.

We can use outlawed needs, desires, and feelings to orientate our radical politics. Rather than just taking needs in general as a given, we should explore needs that are not currently being met, and which therefore constitute a desire for a different world. As these needs and emotions point to a world that is less exploitative, they form a more expansive horizon for politics. Emotion and desire could have a central place in radical politics, as our struggles are bound together through emotional practices. Larne Abse Gogarty and Hannah Proctor, in their essay 'Communist Feelings', argue for the exploration of the emotional worlds of radical politics. Political struggles, they suggest, can involve feelings of both disillusion and comradely love.[55] Thus, we need to be attentive to how emotional relationships are built and sustained in left movements. Being on the left must involve a political commitment to caring for each other outside of the family – we might even say that communism is inherently against the family, insofar as it strives to undo the privatisation of feeling and care-scarcity that the nuclear family form entails and reproduces. Left movements should therefore seek to create more expansive forms of emotional care and investments. Such attention to emotional investments is necessary for left movements to sustain themselves. It is essential that we create spaces where long-term aims and discussions on strategy can co-exist with immediate experiences of joy and care. As Automnia puts it, 'Perhaps we can imagine communism as the elucidation of this warmth and ecstasy, as their emergence from the exceptional into the everyday.'[56]

This concern for feelings and needs can also raise questions of scale. How do we go beyond the worlds of queer and left-wing political cultures to realise a reorganisation of reproduction for everyone? Such a project implies the abolition of waged work, which currently dominates and devalues reproduction and limits our emotional horizons. It also challenges the activity of the welfare state, whose politics of reproduction often involves a normative vision of gendered and sexual relations aimed at reproducing labour power. It would mean a politics that goes beyond patchwork welfare reforms that merely complement unwaged reproductive work in the family. Instead, we need large-scale innovations in housing, city planning, childcare, education, eldercare, and health in order to generalise less oppressive and exploitative forms of reproduction. These interventions would need to resist implicit assumptions of the family as the central site of reproductive work. We need to abandon the notion that the family is necessary or desirable as the centre of reproduction and the social world of needs. Instead, such interventions could help us overcome the 'organized care scarcity' that Lewis sees as essential in upholding family values.[57] As Michèle Barrett and Mary McIntosh suggest, family abolition might be less a project of replacing the family with a new hegemonic social model and more one of making family unnecessary for people's survival through constituting non-familial means of satisfying needs.[58]

Currently, childcare and eldercare are often organised along normative understandings of social property and propriety. A queer framework helps us recognise how these forms of care are regulated through welfare politics and structures of family law. It therefore implies a critique of the state, offering ways of going beyond heteronormative forms of kinship. Over the past decades, a wealth of research surrounding queer kinship has focused on the relation to children. Gay and lesbian people have gone from being considered non-reproductive to being increasingly integrated in legalised forms of reproduction. However, queer parenting often exceeds legitimised forms of legal and biological parenthood, and children are raised by people who are not necessarily recognisable as parents, either in the sense of being 'blood relations' or according to legal models of custody rights.[59] Queer parenting can therefore resist the zero-sum game of emotional exclusivity that structures normative kinship forms and refuse the exclusive, proprietarian logic of heterosexual families, where there can be only one or two people primarily responsible for the emotional care of children.

But parenting practices which exist in heterosexual families, such as adoption, surrogacy, and reliance on nannies and childcare workers, already implicitly question whether a child can only have one mother.[60] A queer critique of reproductive labour can point to these unstable and invisible aspects of the institution of heterosexual reproduction. It explores all the potentials for a different form of reproduction, as well as dependencies on the reproductive labour of various subjects which have had to be excluded and made invisible in order for the heterosexual nuclear family form to become intelligible. A radical queer politics can use those gaps for a politics of multiple and currently unintelligible forms of reproduction.

While queer parenthood has become increasingly familiar and accepted in the mainstream, queer eldercare has been less explored. But eldercare needs to be central to rethinking models of reproduction. Ageing, illness, disability, and death imply a loss of individual autonomy, and can therefore challenge ideals of liberal subjectivity and possessive individualism. Yet ageing is conspicuously absent from much political discourse, including on the left. The elderly have to be removed and made invisible in order for ideals of the productive subject, and the family as the reproduction of life, to become sustainable. Moreover, the social valuation of waged work serves to devalue the lives of the elderly and others who are not productive within the capitalist economy. Old age is made socially invisible, a tendency that is replicated in left-wing political movements and theory.[61] The material organisation of reproduction also facilitates this invisibility of the elderly. Federici writes about how gentrification threatens the forms of working-class community and solidarity that have provided a social and material safety net for elderly people outside the nuclear family.[62] But such sociality can be recreated. The project of queering eldercare can look to less individualised practices of care and support for inspiration for how to go beyond our currently privatised models of sociality and reproduction.

The politics of childcare and eldercare fit together through a more generalised logic of heterosexual temporality and genealogy. As Kath Weston points out, the fear of ageing and dying alone may be a motivating factor behind the decision to have children.[63] Family is one of the few structures that encourage intergenerational care, thus offering some support in an increasingly age-stratified society.[64] Participating in the logic of property, normative family based on generational reproduction therefore functions as a form of insurance against one's future exclusion from reproductive relationships. Capitalist society creates distinct domains for both children and the elderly, separating them from those participating in waged work. A heteronormative model of life under capitalism assumes distinct stages of life, such as childhood, adolescence, young adulthood, middle age, and old age. These correspond to separate phases of waged work and reproductive labour as well as life events such as marriage and childbirth. A queer and communist politics of reproduction must strive for generational integration and the undoing of separate institutions for different age groups.

This political project might proceed from the unmet needs of elderly queer people, who are often isolated from kin and face higher levels of economic precarity.[65] The goal should be to make eldercare and intergenerational solidarity generally accessible, thus counteracting the privatisation of care within kinship structures as well as the abusive and exploitative relations of care within many private and state facilities. It is essential that we move away from a model where having children becomes an investment in one's own future access to care. This could allow for other forms of reproduction, ones less based on property and obligation. Jane Ward writes that seeing children as an investment in the future prevents pleasurable parent–child relations in the present, and obstructs more comradely and non-exclusive forms of childcare.[66] We need to work against forms of childcare that emotionally reproduce class relations. Rather than focusing on childcare and eldercare as separate issues, we should explore how notions and practices of familial descent foreclose alternative forms of care which are less age-segregated and less based on notions of property.

Moving beyond the Family

Forms of care and emotional support that are less proprietarian already exist. In the project of moving beyond the family, we can draw inspiration from the African American tradition of multiple forms of parenting. As Patricia Hill Collins suggests, these models are not exclusively about the care of one's own children but about a form of guardianship of the community as a whole. Othermothering, the practice of being an extra parent of someone else's child, can become community othermothering, a form of political leadership centred on questions of care. These practices, Hill Collins writes, can be invoked as symbols of power, as black traditions of mothering are central in the reproduction of resistance.[67] Community othermothers, Stanlie James suggests, see that problems from which many people suffer can only be solved through collective action.[68] These multiple and overlapping practices of mothering are based on a less proprietarian model, and are geared towards forms of collective political action. Following Alexis Pauline Gumbs, we might distinguish between motherhood as a status of ownership and mothering as a practice.[69] Gumbs draws on Hortense Spillers's writings, which point to the legacy of slavery in practices of black mothering, where the child was not seen as owned by the mother.[70] While these practices stem from histories of extreme oppression and exploitation, they also point to a tradition of resistance and a mode of being that departs from normative logics of care. Rather than relying on exclusive models of kinship, which tend to place the burden of care on one person, they are capable of integrating different people with various needs into caring relationships. They also counteract the individualising logic of care. Othermothering challenges the idea that a lack of care or 'delinquent youths' are the result of individual failure. Instead, it articulates black mothering itself as a resistance to the patriarchal and racist order of the world.

Race is not a static thing but involves processes of racialisation. Racialisation marks certain groups as worthless, which facilitates their constitution as surplus populations – groups excluded from the labour force but simultaneously necessary for the capitalist economy and creating competition between workers.[71] In order to expand our understanding of racialised and working-class resistance, we also need to explore the so-called lumpenproletariat as a political subject.[72] The lumpenproletariat are those members of the working class that cannot access a wage and rely on criminalised forms of survival. O'Brien argues that while Marx and Engels rejected the lumpenproletariat in favour of the industrial proletariat, the working class of their time 'was not a unified, homogeneous proletarian mass disciplined by factory life, but a cacophony of crime and social chaos' – more suggestive of 'Fourier's queer communism than Engels' gravitation to a natural monogamy'.[73] Criminalised modes of survival can be understood as a form of resistance to property and propriety. Informal economies can also create a material context for non-familial modes of solidarity. Learning from these practices of solidarity involves unlearning habitual emotional responses which tend to discount marginalised subjects as political actors. Resistance to our reproduction as labour power thus also implies resistance to the production and demarcation of surplus populations, including resisting the criminalisation and pathologisation of non-normative forms of reproduction rather than agreeing with the state's assessment that these forms of reproduction are lacking. We can look at these modes of survival as models from which we can learn, even though they are shaped and limited by histories of extreme exploitation and violence.

This applies especially to racialised forms of queer reproduction. We should be careful not to romanticise these caring arrangements, which may also contain exploitative labour relations.[74] But they can serve as sources of inspiration from which we can draw selectively. As Chandan Reddy argues, queer, racialised forms of kinship found their cohesion in the damage produced by heteronormative modes of familial reproduction.[75] Stephanie Coontz writes that black families have historically been less likely to institutionalise orphans and the elderly, as these people were instead cared for within extended kinship networks.[76] However, many queer people have been excluded from more expansive forms of kinship. We can understand such exclusions through bell hooks's description of the normativising of black families who come to aspire to white bourgeois subjectivity, and Gumbs's account of the heteronormativising influences of some black nationalist and pro-natalist discourse.[77] Currently marginalised people are not immune to normalising and exclusive modes of kinship but can themselves become participants of the exclusions of normative family values. But negative queer histories and emotions of trauma and exclusion can be productive for alternative models of solidarity and care.

While racialised and queer forms of kinship sometimes appropriate the language of family, Reddy suggests that they do not succumb to the logic of sexuality as privacy, which tends to further isolate queer subjects.[78] The collective queer life of metropolitan cities has historically revolved around criminalised or informal modes of reproduction. These forms of survival are not necessarily mediated through the gendered practices of the state, the wage, or the family.[79] I want to introduce the criminal queer as a figure for political thought. Similar to the figure of the housewife in Wages for Housework writings, the criminal queer is devalued as a result of

exclusion from formal wage economies. This figure also struggles from a position of exclusion from normative familial
structures. If the figure of the proletarian, in Marx's writings,
only owns his capacity to labour, the criminal queer owns
even less. Throughout this book, I have pointed to the conditions that underlie the white, male, heterosexual proletarian's
capacity to labour – conditions from which the criminal queer
is excluded. This produces a lifeworld often marked by mental
and physical illness, imprisonment, and death. But it also
allows us to glimpse traces of a different form of sociality and
solidarity, as communities are created to protect their members
from various forms of violence. This particular form of
lumpenproletariat, we might speculate, may be politically
important, as it simultaneously fulfils and exceeds the demands
of capital.[80] Because these groups have little to lose, they often
lead the way for revolutionary struggle. This does not mean
that the criminal queer should be positioned as *the* revolutionary subject; it means that our political movements need to
make space for the needs and experiences that stem from
exclusion from both productive and normatively reproductive
spheres.

One example of this practice was Street Transvestite Action
Revolutionaries (STAR), a group of trans, queer, and gender
non-conforming people of colour founded in 1970 in New
York by Sylvia Rivera and Marsha P. Johnson. Simultaneously
an activist group and a collective based on reproductive
labour, STAR provided housing, food, emotional support,
prisoner solidarity, and advocacy for the black and brown
trans community.[81] For young trans people of colour who had
been turned away by their families, Rivera and Johnson
offered a place to sleep in the STAR house. The group also
extended some forms of care to the local community, including free food and childcare. STAR relied on criminalised
means of reproduction – paying the rent with money from sex
work and feeding its members through shoplifting.[82] There is

a link between socially outlawed needs and emotions and acts which are actually criminalised. The desire for a different world is intimately tied to an economy of criminalised practices to satisfy needs.

Weeks suggests that these queer and racialised forms of reproduction constitute a form of self-valorisation, a selective practice of immanent resistance that allows us to constitute new collective subjectivities.[83] STAR understood themselves as engaging in a revolutionary practice, explicitly politicising their needs and desires. They also supported and intervened in various political movements, such as gay, feminist, and antiracist movements.[84] In their practice of reproduction, they used many of the tools advocated by Wages for Housework, including shoplifting, or 'proletarian shopping', and collective housing for those who had been harmed by nuclear families.[85] In the Wages for Housework literature, such practices figure as a form of sabotage on the site of consumption, asserting the power of the proletariat to intervene in reproduction despite the threat of state violence. This project will only be successful if we create collective ways of protecting and caring for one another.

STAR did not mimic white heteronormative notions of the domestic sphere, but rather provided an unstable and flexible definition of home, where there is no clear separation between the domestic space and the community. While these arrangements are limited by various material constraints, and do not constitute ideal forms, they still provide practical examples for how to struggle for better, less exclusionary reproductive arrangements. Through engaging in criminalised economies, they also exist at least partially outside gendered distinctions between production and reproduction and public and private spheres.

Groups such as STAR present challenges for how to sustain and generalise alternative forms of reproduction. The STAR house was a relatively short-lived experiment, and the untimely deaths of its founders show the need for a continued struggle for the survival of trans women of colour. Yet it can map out some directions for organising on the site of reproduction. Such organising, as Lauren Berlant and Michael Warner show, is frequently dismissed as being merely engaged with lifestyle. By contrast, they refer to it as a queer public culture or a world-making project

> where 'world', like 'public', differs from community or group because it necessarily includes more people than can be identified, more spaces than can be mapped beyond a few reference points, modes of feeling that can be learned rather than experienced as a birthright.[86]

They criticise attempts to portray gay and lesbian movements as struggles for recognition, the opposite of class-based demands for redistribution. Berlant and Warner assert that to understand the queer politics of world-making 'only as self-expression or as a demand for recognition would be to misrecognize the fundamentally unequal material conditions whereby the institutions of social reproduction are coupled to the forms of hetero culture'.[87] These projects of world-making are a necessary aspect of a radical politics which strives to uncouple social reproduction from both heterosexuality and capitalist institutions. Their limitations can in themselves be instructive for new directions for struggle. For example, difficulty in scaling up these projects owing to lack of suitable housing can lead us to struggle for the provision of affordable or free homes that do not assume a normative family model or individualising modes of property ownership. Free and decent housing is an important aspect of reconfiguring reproduction, which can help us expand the horizon of reproductive needs. We can also address the working conditions of reproductive labour in terms of free access to adequate public spaces, transport, and reproductive services, thus extending beyond the private sphere towards a project of world-making.

When considering the direction of an emancipatory politics of reproduction, it is worth asking what demands would facilitate non-normative forms of reproduction and ensure the survival and wellbeing of those currently most marginalised. In this way, queer politics and theory can become less concerned with anti-normativity as a goal in itself and more concerned with overcoming the material constraints that currently hinder a different future. This might be a daunting task, as there are presently many structures that limit more emancipatory forms of reproduction. But it is necessary to keep searching for the limits that currently curtail a liberatory reproductive politics, and struggle to surpass those limits. This also means that there is no one site that can be privileged in struggling for a better future – reproductive struggles must be waged in a number of different sites and call for a politics of coalition between variously marginalised and exploited groups. These coalitions would need to start from the principle of unity on the basis of the needs and desires of the most precarious and oppressed groups rather than on false universality on the basis of the perceived interest of the majority. Such politics, as James suggests, would strengthen the working class by giving increased power and visibility to its most marginalised members, combining struggles against oppression with those against exploitation and economic precarity.[88] This is a necessary part of undoing the subjective and emotional hierarchies that currently structure left politics as well as society more broadly.

Material conditions of work are tightly imbricated with subjective structures of emotional reproduction. O'Brien describes her family-abolitionist vision as

> communes of a couple hundred people who pool reproductive labor and share in child-rearing, include some attention to sexual pleasure and fulfillment, and work to meet everyone's interpersonal and development needs without barring chosen affective, romantic or parental bonds between individuals.[89]

Here, the housing unit serves as the material condition for affective needs and desires. It combines needs for various types of care with the desire for sexual and emotional satisfaction. This type of project would both represent and require a large-scale challenge to the current organisation of reproduction, reorganising housing, work, care, and sociality. Contemporary feminist politics can learn from the visions of the history of materialist feminist intervention in collective reproduction, such as attempts to collectivise the provision of cooked meals and build housing that includes space for collective child-care.[90] While many of these projects were severely limited in various ways, they share the belief that the domestic is not a static unit but something that can and must be changed in order for society to change.

New Horizons of Feeling

It is important, then, to think about the material conditions for new forms of sociality. Social bonds are always based on various structures of work and living, and our ideas about how sociality should work in turn impact how we organise our work and domestic lives. In his investigation of the politics of friendship, Alan Sears notes that the current organisation of waged work, together with increased pressures on families to provide unwaged care work, leaves little time for pleasurable interactions with friends. The relatively low level of commodification of friendship compared to romantic or familial attachments means that friendship is currently being increasingly marginalised in our lives.[91] Focusing on such constraints might enable a radical politics of friendship to emerge. Friendship, and other non-kinship forms of sociality, are neither on the side of the family nor on the side of waged work. A politics which seeks to remodel sociality beyond the boundaries of private and public, and beyond the spheres of waged work and family life, might do well in exploring the queer potentials of a politics of friendship. This queer history predates the emergence of stable lesbian and gay identities, emerging in nineteenth-century cultures of romantic friendship in which same-sex intimacy could flourish.[92] As Weston points out in her study of 'chosen family', queer people have often created intimate networks where there is little symbolic differentiation between erotic and non-erotic ties or friends and family. As it crosses lines of households, chosen family is also a means of undoing boundaries between the public and private.[93] Family abolition is a politics of friendship.

It is in this context of public intimacy and queer world-making that we should be wary of the mainstream LGBT movement's turn to a politics of love. Rather than politicising emotion, the now-commonplace slogan 'love is love' serves to privatise queer erotic and emotional bonds in the name of romance. Such focus tends to erase the specificity of queer life in favour of a political argument based on the purported emotional similarity of queer and heterosexual lives. While this political focus has undoubtedly brought material benefits to many gay and lesbian couples, it is part of a more generalised attack on the possibilities of queer world-making. Such privatisation of feeling is part and parcel of the privatisation of care under neoliberal regimes.[94] What we need is not an expanded and more inclusive understanding of romantic love. Instead, we need to counter the organisation of life that makes romance and familial ties the precondition for access to emotional and material forms of care and resources. For example, Melinda Cooper's account of ACT UP underscores how their AIDS activism sought to detach access to care from privatised models of family responsibility and employment.[95] Exclusive familial bonds are reproduced through law and models of property. A contemporary queer politics of reproduction could disrupt these social forms through the creation of alternative modes of emotional support which enable us to live and struggle outside of the family. Such politics could centre on friendship as a more open form of relationality, which could potentially traverse generational boundaries as well as allow for more expansive constructions of intimacy. A focus on friendship could also tell us something about how to remodel caring relationships in more comradely ways, in which care is not based on bonds defined according to legal or biological standards.[96] The figure of the comrade might also help us reorient our desires away from the family. Comradeship allows for more expansive forms of intimacy and emotional practices based on solidarity rather than privatised attachments.

Queer Marxist feminist Rosemary Hennessy has suggested that the concept of love should be reclaimed as the name for 'an affect-culture of collaboration and passionate reason that accompanies the conversion of living labor into organized resistance'.[97] Her project is close to those of Alexandra Kollontai and Firestone, who both argue for the generalisation of feelings currently reserved for romantic intimacy.[98] Hennessy re-articulates love as a collective political practice. Weeks similarly articulates a politics built on forms of laughter, where ironic and joyful laughter can articulate a politics against ressentiment, which she understands in terms of the reduction of capacity for action.[99]

I appreciate Weeks's and Hennessy's emphasis on affective cultures linked to collective resistance. However, I have argued for a politics where negative feelings are not necessarily understood as capacity-reducing. Rather, in a politics against normative patterns of emotional reproduction, it is necessary to reclaim some of the bad feelings that emotional labour most often serves to manage and outlaw. Good feeling, including love, is often what reduces our capacity for action. This is not to say that left movements need to discard all positive feelings. It is crucial that we make time and space for joy in our organising efforts. But moments of joy, unlike the more all-encompassing notion of happiness, can co-exist with feelings that have been deemed bad or inappropriate. There can be something very joyful in being angry together. The reclamation of outlaw feelings increases the width of our affective capacity, and makes radical use of those feelings that are seen as bad or harmful. This also implies the degendering of feeling, where currently gender-coded emotions become accessible to everyone.

The emotion of love is overburdened with meanings of romantic and familial intimacy and exclusivity in a way that makes it difficult to reclaim for a more collective project. It is especially closely associated with demands for privatised arrangements of care and emotional labour. Love undermines solidarity. In our society, it has been reserved for the intimate sphere of coupledom and family – it is seen as hard to find and jealously guarded. The emotional practice of solidarity is the opposite of the zero-sum game of romantic and familial love. Solidarity means precisely going beyond caring for those to whom we have an emotional attachment to build a lifeworld of intimate strangers.

A political project of refusing emotional reproduction must strive to make sociality less like work by freeing it from current constraints. Emotion becomes labour through its privatisation and individualisation. These conditions can be refused and resisted. Gendered work is not something that we can simply choose to step outside of but is dependent on material constraints and structures of (re)production. Within these forms of gendered work, however, there is some scope for creative forms of resistance, and through collectivising and denaturalising reproductive labour it can become labour for ourselves rather than for capital. Such labour could also entail playing or experimenting with different forms of sociality without denying that these experiments depend on labour. As the writings of Wages Due Lesbians show, reproductive labour is not automatically free when performed in the context of queer relationships, yet it does not necessarily carry with it the reproduction of the same coercive structures and forms of devaluation of the labouring subject. It can be geared towards producing outlawed pleasure and power. As Ruth Hall puts it, 'Our ability to live without men, our ability to express ourselves and our feelings for each other are in turn a source of power.'[100] Power and freedom are thus not individualised but rather understood within the context of relations of shared labour and care as well as a commitment to a politics of reproducing against capital's normativising tendencies.

Interventions into alternative forms of reproduction and gendered being do not automatically allow us to step outside the sphere of work, but might position that work differently within dominant and coercive structures. Queerness, historically lacking ties to the privatised sphere of the family and the normative gender formations produced through waged work, might offer some tools for inventing different forms of emotional care – one which can challenge some of the boundaries that currently restrict emotional experience.

Queerness also offers tools for politicising intimacy so that it no longer appears as naturally given or the result of instinctive emotional bonds between family members. For this project, we can also draw on a long history of working-class sociality outside the family. Coontz argues that in the early twentieth century, 'the idea that the family and the sexual division of labour were presocial and sacrosanct imparted a new sense of both privacy and universality to family life and gender roles'.[101] Before that, however, these ideas were not widespread among the working class, and working-class sociality was less anchored in familial forms. A project of remaking reproduction could therefore draw on a long history of working-class sociality as well as new and creative modes of being together. Queerness can produce subjectivities that are not understood as pre-social but rather emerge as already political. Sociality and emotional bonds then come to have an immediate political and collective character, which can be mobilised for practices of solidarity and coalition-building. There is no strict boundary between the political and the pleasure of intimate connections. Queerness as a form of political subjectivity can draw on the experience of public forms of feeling, as well as acquired skills for emotional labour, in order to undo the distinction posited by capitalist constructions of public and private. By using modes of work and play, emotional practices can be turned against the coercive management of feeling, and instead use our acquired emotional skill to experiment with new forms of sociality.

This requires that we try to undo the practices of individualism that structure much of our daily lives. Emotional labour is essential for creating individualised modes of subjectivity, which also requires that such labour remains invisible. But as Lewis writes, 'We are the makers of one another. And we could learn collectively to act like it.'[102] Similarly, Cynthia Dewi Oka argues that we need to become 'encumbered with and responsible for each other'.[103] These ways of relating to other people would require the undoing of the invisible dependency of individualism on various forms of reproductive labour. Challenging current forms of emotional labour could threaten individualism, and conversely the refusal of affective individualism would lessen the need for emotional labour. We could move towards forms of non-sovereign relationality. For Berlant, this will involve 'unlearning the expectations of sovereignty as self-possession, a mechanism for control and evidence of freedom'.[104] Experimentation into new forms of being together would have to search for new forms of freedom through collective subjectivity. When we no longer posit individualism as a precondition of freedom, we can recognise that it is produced through coercive forms of labour.

Here, it is useful to turn to Weeks's reformulation of feminist standpoints as collective forms of subjectivity constituted by labour which selectively draw on the histories and practices available to them.[105] Rather than affirming or valorising feminised work or emotional labour, we can use historical examples of practices and modes of being to both denaturalise and mobilise particular capacities. I have briefly sketched some modes of alternative sociality which provide directions for new social forms through challenging the boundaries that currently limit these practices. We can also selectively draw from historical examples of different modes of being, including working-class life in the nineteenth and early twentieth century, where boundaries between private and public were not drawn as rigidly as in later versions of working-class sociality. Marginalised and surplus populations, who never had access to the forms of institutional security that came to dominate working-class sociality in the post-war era, continue to carry this legacy today, despite or because of significant hardship. There is a link between these forms of sociality and the project of reclaiming social wealth, the means of production, and access to space and free time. Forms of solidarity and care depend on appropriate spatial and material conditions. Conversely, the politics of reclaiming material wealth cannot do without a focus on the emotional dimensions of ownership and belonging, and how these need to change in the process of creating more liveable futures. Radical politics has to include an emphasis on emotional reproduction and social life, and we must assume that our current forms of sociality will be transformed within the process of transforming society.

Notes

Introduction

1 Sarah Jaffe, *Work Won't Love You Back: How Devotion to Our Jobs Keeps Us Exploited, Exhausted and Alone*, Hurst, 2021, 32.
2 Arlie Russell Hochschild, *The Managed Heart: Commercialization of Human Feeling*, University of California Press, 2003, 165.
3 Sophie Lewis, *Full Surrogacy Now: Feminism against Family*, Verso, 2019, 59.
4 Silvia Federici and Arlen Austin, eds., *The New York Wages for Housework Committee, 1972–1977: History, Theory and Documents*, Autonomedia, 2017, 16.
5 Silvia Federici, *Revolution at Point Zero: Housework, Reproduction, and Feminist Struggle*, PM Press, 2012, 16.
6 Lewis, *Full Surrogacy Now*, 125.
7 Federici, *Revolution at Point Zero*, 16, 20.

1. Emotional Reproduction

1 Sara Ahmed, *The Promise of Happiness*, Duke University Press, 2010.
2 Alison Jaggar, 'Love and Knowledge: Emotion in Feminist Epistemology', in *Women and Reason*, ed. Elizabeth Harvey and Kathleen Okruhlik, University of Michigan Press, 1992, 123–4.
3 Agnes Heller, *A Theory of Emotions*, Goreum, 1979, 7.
4 Kathi Weeks, *Constituting Feminist Subjects*, Cornell University Press, 1998, 133.
5 Arlie Russell Hochschild, *The Managed Heart: Commercialization of Human Feeling*, University of California Press, 2003, 7.
6 Raymond Williams, *Marxism and Literature*, Oxford University Press, 1977, 132.
7 Hochschild, *The Managed Heart*, 34.
8 Cinzia Arruzza, 'The Capitalism of Affects', *Public Seminar*, 25 August 2014, publicseminar.org.

9   Lawrence Stone, *The Family, Sex and Marriage in England, 1500–1800*, Penguin, 1979, 151.

10 Deborah Lupton, *The Emotional Self: A Sociocultural Exploration*, Sage, 1998, 72.

11 Teresa Brennan, *The Transmission of Affect*, Cornell University Press, 2004, 2; Brenna Bhandar, *Colonial Lives of Property: Law, Land, and Racial Regimes of Ownership*, Duke University Press, 2018, 4, 179.

12 Arruzza, 'The Capitalism of Affects'.

13 Johanna Oksala, 'Affective Labor and Feminist Politics', *Signs: Journal of Women in Culture and Society* 41(2), 2016, 295.

14 Marjorie DeVault, *Feeding the Family: The Social Organization of Caring as Gendered Work*, University of Chicago Press, 1991, 35; Christopher Carrington, *No Place like Home: Relationships and Family Life among Lesbians and Gay Men*, University of Chicago Press, 1999, 32–3.

15 Anne Boyer, *The Undying: A Meditation on Modern Illness*, Allen Lane, 2019, 125.

16 Hochschild, *The Managed Heart*, 84.

17 Micaela Di Leonardo, 'The Female World of Cards and Holidays: Women, Families, and the Work of Kinship', *Signs: Journal of Women in Culture and Society* 12(3), 1987, 442; Brenda Seery and Sue Crowley, 'Women's Emotion Work in the Family: Relationship Management and the Process of Building Father-Child Relationships', *Journal of Family Issues* 21(1), 2000, 110.

18 Lawrence Stone, *Family, Sex and Marriage*, 180.

19 Leopoldina Fortunati, *The Arcane of Reproduction: Housework, Prostitution, Labor and Capital*, Autonomedia, 1995, 110.

20 Giovanna Franca Dalla Costa, *The Work of Love: Unpaid Housework, Poverty and Sexual Violence at the Dawn of the 21st Century*, Autonomedia, 2008, 53.

21 Ibid., 57.

22 Wendy Edmond and Suzie Fleming, eds., *All Work and No Pay: Women, Housework, and the Wages Due*, Falling Wall Press, 1975, 73.

23 Hochschild, *The Managed Heart*, 68.

24 Lauren Berlant, 'Cruel Optimism', *Differences: A Journal of Feminist Cultural Studies* 17(3), 2006, 21.

25 Lauren Berlant, *Desire/Love*, Punctum Books, 2012, 102.

26 Hochschild, *The Managed Heart*, 236; Brennan, *The Transmission of Affect*, 32.

27 DeVault, *Feeding the Family*, 85, 90.

28 Jane Ward, 'Gender Labor: Transmen, Femmes, and Collective Work of Transgression', *Sexualities* 13(2), 2010.

29 Sophie Lewis, 'How Domestic Labor Robs Women of Their Love', *Boston Review*, 28 October 2021, bostonreview.net.

30 Dalla Costa, *The Work of Love*, 46, 88.

31 Edmond and Fleming, *All Work and No Pay*, 73; Cameron Lynne Macdonald, *Shadow Mothers: Nannies, Au Pairs, and the Micropolitics of Mothering*, University of California Press, 2010, 28.

32 Sharon Hays, *The Cultural Contradictions of Motherhood*, Yale University Press, 1996, 150–1; Hochschild, *The Managed Heart*, 82.

33 DeVault, *Feeding the Family*, 134.

34 Silvia Federici, 'On Affective Labor', in *Cognitive Capitalism, Education, and Digital Labor*, ed. Michael Peters and Ergin Bulut, Peter Lang, 2011, 69.

35 Michèle Barrett and Mary McIntosh, *The Anti-social Family*, Verso, 2015, 80.

36 Hochschild, *The Managed Heart*, 85.

37 Stone, *Family, Sex and Marriage*, 149.

38 Francesca Cancian, *Love in America: Gender and Self-Development*, Cambridge University Press, 1987, 18; Hays, *Cultural Contradictions of Motherhood*, 125.

39 Viviana Zelizer, *Pricing the Priceless Child: The Changing Social Value of Children*, Basic Books, 1985, 3.

40 Hays, *Cultural Contradictions of Motherhood*, 32.

41 Ibid., 55; Brennan, *The Transmission of Affect*, 32.

42 Arlie Russell Hochschild, *The Second Shift: Working Parents and the Revolution at Home*, Viking, 1989, 150.

43 Hays, *Cultural Contradictions of Motherhood*, 3–43.

44 Macdonald, *Shadow Mothers*, 13.

45 Seery and Crowley, 'Women's Emotion Work', 122.

46 Hochschild, *The Managed Heart*, 69.

47 Bonnie Fox, 'Motherhood as a Class Act: The Many Ways in Which "Intensive Mothering" Is Entangled with Social Class', in *Social Reproduction: Feminist Political Economy Challenges Neo-liberalism*, ed. Meg Luxton and Kate Bezanson, McGill-Queen's Press, 2006, 237.

48 Fortunati, *The Arcane of Reproduction*, 75.

49 Brennan, *The Transmission of Affect*, 32.

50 Hochschild, *The Managed Heart*, 157.

51 Macdonald, *Shadow Mothers*, 21, 25.

52 Ibid., 203.

53 Dorothy Roberts, 'Spiritual and Menial Housework', *Yale Journal of Law and Feminism* 9, 1997, 57, 59.

54 Hays, *Cultural Contradictions of Motherhood*, 29.

55 Roberts, 'Spiritual and Menial Housework', 52.

56 Hays, *Cultural Contradictions of Motherhood*, 29.

57 Hochschild, *The Managed Heart*, 158.

58 Ibid., 156.

59 Silvia Federici, *Revolution at Point Zero: Housework, Reproduction, and Feminist Struggle*, PM Press, 2012, 31.

60 Fortunati, *The Arcane of Reproduction*, 75.

61 Stephanie Coontz, *The Social Origins of Private Life: A History of American Families, 1600–1900*, Verso, 1988, 295.

62 Maya Gonzalez and Jeanne Neton, 'The Logic of Gender', *Endnotes* 3, 2013, 62.

63 Michael Hardt and Antonio Negri, *Empire*, Harvard University Press, 2000, 294.

64 Federici, *Revolution at Point Zero*, 107.

65 Hochschild, *The Managed Heart*, 150; Macdonald, *Shadow Mothers*, 114.

66 Emma Dowling, 'Producing the Dining Experience: Measure, Subjectivity and the Affective Worker', *Ephemera: Theory and Politics in Organization* 7(1), 2007, 122.

67 Federici, 'On Affective Labor', 69.

68 Kathi Weeks, 'Life within and against Work: Affective Labor, Feminist Critique, and Post-Fordist Politics', *Ephemera: Theory and Politics in Organization* 7(1), 2007, 241; Weeks, *The Problem with Work: Feminism, Marxism, Antiwork Politics, and Postwork Imaginaries*, Duke University Press, 2011, 73.

69 Hochschild, *The Managed Heart*, 97.

70 Steve Taylor and Melissa Tyler, 'Emotional Labour and Sexual Difference in the Airline Industry', *Work, Employment, and Society* 14(1), 2000, 83.

71 Hochschild, *The Managed Heart*, 119–20.

72 Robin Leidner, *Fast Food, Fast Talk: Service Work and the Routinization of Everyday Life*, University of California Press, 1993, 5.

73 Emma Dowling, *The Care Crisis: What Caused It and How Can We End It?*, Verso, 2021, 102.

74 Sharon Bolton, *Emotion Management in the Workplace*, Bloomsbury Publishing, 2005, 97.

75 Rebecca Selberg, *Femininity at Work: Gender, Labour, and Changing Relations of Power in a Swedish Hospital*, Arkiv förlag, 2012, 73, 223.

76 Arlie Russell Hochschild, *The Commercialization of Intimate Life: Notes from Home and Work*, University of California Press, 2003, 24; emphasis in original.

77 Barrett and McIntosh, *The Anti-social Family*, 47, 80.

78 Silvia Federici and Nicole Cox, 'Counter-planning from the Kitchen', in Federici, *Revolution at Point Zero*, 35.

79 Encarnación Gutiérrez-Rodríguez, *Migration, Domestic Work and Affect: A Decolonial Approach on Value and the Feminization of Labor*, Routledge, 2010, 4.

80 Federici, 'On Affective Labor', 67; Federici, *Revolution at Point Zero*, 49.

81 Camille Barbagallo, 'The Political Economy of Reproduction: Motherhood, Work and the Home in Neoliberal Britain', PhD thesis, University of East London, 2016, 129.

2. The Political Economy of Love

1 Ruth Schwartz Cowan, *More Work for Mother: The Ironies of Household Technology from the Open Hearth to the Microwave*, Basic Books, 1983.

2 Silvia Federici, *Revolution at Point Zero: Housework, Reproduction, and Feminist Struggle*, PM Press, 2012, 47.

3 Emma Dowling, *The Care Crisis: What Caused It and How Can We End It?*, Verso, 2021, 193.

4 Silvia Federici and Arlen Austin, eds., *The New York Wages for Housework Committee, 1972–1977: History, Theory and Documents*, Autonomedia, 2017, 91.

5 Federici, *Revolution at Point Zero*, 17.

6 Federici and Austin, *New York Wages for Housework*, 74.

7 Karl Marx, *Capital: A Critique of Political Economy*, vol. 1, Penguin, 1990, 270.

8 Leopoldina Fortunati, *The Arcane of Reproduction: Housework, Prostitution, Labor and Capital*, Autonomedia, 1995, 165.

9 Federici, *Revolution at Point Zero*, 99.

10 Wendy Edmond and Suzie Fleming, eds., *All Work and No Pay: Women, Housework, and the Wages Due*, Falling Wall Press, 1975, 83.

11 Nona Glazer, *Women's Paid and Unpaid Labor: The Work Transfer in Health Care and Retailing*, Temple University Press, 1993, xi; Maya Gonzalez and Jeanne Neton, 'The Logic of Gender', *Endnotes* 3, 2013, 86.

12 Federici, *Revolution at Point Zero*, 104.

13 Evelyn Nakano Glenn, 'The Social Construction and Institutionalization of Gender and Race', in *Revisioning Gender*, ed. Myra Marx Ferree, Judith Lorber, and Beth Hess, Sage, 1999, 19.

14 Ruth Wilson Gilmore, *Golden Gulag: Prisons, Surplus, Crisis, and Opposition in Globalizing California*, University of California Press, 2007, 28.

15 Melissa Wright, *Disposable Women and Other Myths of Global Capitalism*, Routledge, 2006, 18.

16 Wilmette Brown, 'Black Women's Struggle against Sterilization', unpublished manuscript, box 1, Wages for Housework Special Collections, Lesbian Herstory Archive, New York, 1976, 3, 15.

17 Francie Wyland, *Child Custody, Motherhood, Lesbianism*, Wages for Housework Action Group, 1976, 4.

18 Mariarosa Dalla Costa, *Family, Welfare, and the State: Between Progressivism and the New Deal*, Common Notions, 2015, 20.

19 Ibid., 91, 94.

20 Melinda Cooper, *Family Values: Between Neoliberalism and the New Social Conservatism*, Zone Books, 2017, 9.

21 Marx, *Capital*, 521.

22 Fortunati, *The Arcane of Reproduction*, 172.

23 Stephanie Coontz, *The Social Origins of Private Life: A History of American Families, 1600–1900*, Verso, 1988, 215; Dorothy Roberts, 'Spiritual and Menial Housework', *Yale Journal of Law and Feminism* 9, 1997, 55–9.

24 Fortunati, *The Arcane of Reproduction*, 157–8.

25 Ibid., 15.

26 Ibid., 129–30.

27 Federici, *Revolution at Point Zero*, 23.

28 David Eng, *The Feeling of Kinship: Queer Liberalism and the Racialization of Intimacy*, Duke University Press, 2010, 43.

29 Edmond and Fleming, *All Work and No Pay*, 83.

30 Kathi Weeks, *Constituting Feminist Subjects*, Cornell University Press, 1998, 136.

31 Kathi Weeks, 'Life within and against Work: Affective Labor, Feminist Critique, and Post-Fordist Politics', *Ephemera: Theory and Politics in Organization* 7(1), 2007, 248.

32 Brown, 'Black Women's Struggle', 19.

33 Silvia Federici, *Re-enchanting the World: Feminism and the Politics of the Commons*, PM Press, 2018, 62.

34 Mariarosa Dalla Costa, *The Power of Women and the Subversion of the Community*, Falling Wall Press, 1972, 25; Selma James, *Sex, Race and Class: The Perspective of Winning*, PM Press, 2012, 66.

35 Marx, *Capital*, 341, 429.

36 Bridget Anderson, *Doing the Dirty Work? The Global Politics of Domestic Labour*, Zed Books, 2000; Sara Farris, *In the Name of Women's Rights: The Rise of Femonationalism*, Duke University Press, 2017.

37 James, *Sex, Race and Class*, 81.

38 Federici, *Revolution at Point Zero*, 39.

39 Edmond and Fleming, *All Work and No Pay*, 88.

3. Gendering Work

1 Shiloh Whitney, 'Byproductive Labor: A Feminist Theory of Affective Labor beyond the Productive–Reproductive Distinction', *Philosophy & Social Criticism* 44(6), 2018, 645.
2 Silvia Federici, *Revolution at Point Zero: Housework, Reproduction, and Feminist Struggle*, PM Press, 2012, 8.
3 Silvia Federici, *Caliban and the Witch: Women, the Body and Primitive Accumulation*, Autonomedia, 2004, 115, 135; Federici, *Revolution at Point Zero*, 37.
4 Wilmette Brown, 'The Autonomy of Black Lesbian Women', unpublished manuscript, box 1, Wages for Housework Special Collections, Lesbian Herstory Archive, New York, 1976, 4.
5 Federici, *Revolution at Point Zero*, 16.
6 Kathi Weeks, *Constituting Feminist Subjects*, Cornell University Press, 1998, 124–33.
7 Carin Holmberg, *Det kallas kärlek: En socialpsykologisk studie om kvinnors underordning och mäns överordning bland unga jämställda par*, Anamma, 1993, 158; Kevin Floyd, *The Reification of Desire: Toward a Queer Marxism*, University of Minnesota Press, 2009, 99.
8 Diemut Elisabet Bubeck, *Care, Gender, and Justice*, Clarendon Press, 1995, 183.
9 Karl Marx, *Capital: A Critique of Political Economy*, vol. 1, Penguin, 1990, 344–8.
10 Dorothy Roberts, 'Spiritual and Menial Housework', *Yale Journal of Law and Feminism* 9, 1997, 77.
11 Giovanna Franca Dalla Costa, *The Work of Love: Unpaid Housework, Poverty and Sexual Violence at the Dawn of the 21st Century*, Autonomedia, 2008, 54.
12 Federici, *Revolution at Point Zero*, 25.
13 Melissa Wright, *Disposable Women and Other Myths of Global Capitalism*, Routledge, 2006, 74; Dalla Costa, *The Work of Love*, 71.
14 Silvia Federici and Arlen Austin, eds., *The New York Wages for Housework Committee, 1972–1977: History, Theory and Documents*, Autonomedia, 2017, 129.
15 Wilmette Brown, 'Black Women's Struggle against Sterilization', unpublished manuscript, box 1, Wages for Housework Special Collections, Lesbian Herstory Archive, New York, 1976, 8.
16 Wendy Edmond and Suzie Fleming, eds., *All Work and No Pay: Women, Housework, and the Wages Due*, Falling Wall Press, 1975, 24.

17 Louise Toupin, *Wages for Housework: A History of an International Feminist Movement, 1972–77*, Pluto Press, 2018, 107.

18 Nancy Fraser and Linda Gordon, 'A Genealogy of "Dependency": Tracing a Keyword of the US Welfare State', in Nancy Fraser, *Fortunes of Feminism: From State-Managed Capitalism to Neoliberal Crisis*, Verso, 2011, 91, 94.

19 C. B. Macpherson, *The Political Theory of Possessive Individualism: Hobbes to Locke*, Clarendon Press, 1962, 3.

20 Marx, *Capital*, 164ff.

21 Fraser and Gordon, 'A Genealogy of "Dependency"', 94.

22 Stephanie Coontz, *The Way We Never Were: American Families and the Nostalgia Trap*, Basic Books, 1992, 53; emphasis in original.

23 Arlie Russell Hochschild, *The Managed Heart: Commercialization of Human Feeling*, University of California Press, 2003, 166.

24 Stephanie Shields, *Speaking from the Heart: Gender and the Social Meaning of Emotion*, Cambridge University Press, 2002, 9, 38.

25 Michèle Barrett and Mary McIntosh, *The Anti-social Family*, Verso, 2015, 47.

26 Melinda Cooper, *Family Values: Between Neoliberalism and the New Social Conservatism*, Zone Books, 2017, 57–8.

27 Christopher Carrington, *No Place like Home: Relationships and Family Life among Lesbians and Gay Men*, University of Chicago Press, 1999, 193, 200, 222.

28 Joan Acker, 'Hierarchies, Jobs, Bodies: A Theory of Gendered Organizations', *Gender & Society* 4(2), 1990, 150.

29 Hochschild, *The Managed Heart*, 170.

30 Maya Gonzalez and Jeanne Neton, 'The Logic of Gender', *Endnotes* 3, 2013, 76.

31 Michelle Budig, Joya Misra, and Irene Böckmann, 'The Motherhood Penalty in Cross-National Perspective: The Importance of Work–Family Policies and Cultural Attitudes', *Social Politics* 19(2), 2012.

32 Dorothy Roberts, *Killing the Black Body: Race, Reproduction, and the Meaning of Liberty*, Pantheon Books, 1997, 33.

33 Roberts, 'Spiritual and Menial Housework', 62.

34 Margaret Prescod, 'Bringing It All Back Home', in Margaret Prescod and Norma Steele, *Black Women: Bringing It All Back Home*, Falling Wall Press, 1980, 14.

35 Coontz, *The Way We Never Were*, 53.

36 Floyd, *The Reification of Desire*, 95.

37 Weeks, *Constituting Feminist Subjects*, 133.

38 Cynthia Cockburn, *Brothers: Male Dominance and Technological Change*, Westview Press, 1983, 204.

39 Selma James, *Sex, Race and Class: The Perspective of Winning*, PM Press, 2012, 96.
40 Barrett and McIntosh, *The Anti-social Family*, 145.
41 Kate Mulholland, 'Gender Power and Property Relations within Entrepreneurial Wealthy Families', *Gender, Work and Organization* 3(2), 1996, 114.
42 Coontz, *The Way We Never Were*, 63.
43 Hochschild, *The Managed Heart*, 132, 167.
44 Ibid., 105.
45 Leopoldina Fortunati, *The Arcane of Reproduction: Housework, Prostitution, Labor and Capital*, Autonomedia, 1995, 77.
46 Silvia Federici and Nicole Cox, 'Counter-planning from the Kitchen', in Federici, *Revolution at Point Zero*, 32.
47 Fraser and Gordon, 'A Genealogy of "Dependency"', 109–10.
48 Ibid., 99.
49 James, *Sex, Race and Class*, 96.
50 Sara Ahmed, *The Promise of Happiness*, Duke University Press, 2010.
51 Fortunati, *The Arcane of Reproduction*, 75.
52 Federici, *Revolution at Point Zero*, 24.
53 Lauren Berlant, *Desire/Love*, Punctum Books, 2012, 21.
54 Hochschild, *The Managed Heart*, 163.
55 Federici, *Revolution at Point Zero*, 17.
56 Mariarosa Dalla Costa, *The Power of Women and the Subversion of the Community*, Falling Wall Press, 1972, 40.
57 Fortunati, *The Arcane of Reproduction*, 110.
58 Brenda Seery and Sue Crowley, 'Women's Emotion Work in the Family: Relationship Management and the Process of Building Father-Child Relationships', *Journal of Family Issues* 21(1), 2000.
59 Hochschild, *The Managed Heart*, 168.
60 Pamela Fishman, 'Interaction: The Work Women Do', *Social Problems* 25(4), 1978, 402.
61 Holmberg, *Det kallas kärlek*, 188.
62 Hochschild, *The Managed Heart*, 167.
63 Ibid., 173.
64 Ibid., 169.
65 Ibid., 169.
66 Shields, *Speaking from the Heart*, 53.
67 Jean Duncombe and Dennis Marsden, 'Love and Intimacy: The Gender Division of Emotion and "Emotion Work": A Neglected Aspect of Sociological Discussion of Heterosexual Relationships', *Sociology* 27(2), 1993, 236.

68 Tamsin Wilton, 'Sisterhood in the Service of Patriarchy: Heterosexual Women's Friendships and Male Power', *Feminism & Psychology* 2(3), 1992, 507.

69 Hochschild, *The Managed Heart*, 174.

70 Whitney, 'Byproductive Labor', 643.

71 Hochschild, *The Managed Heart*, 6, 178.

72 Whitney, 'Byproductive Labor', 639.

73 Holmberg, *Det kallas kärlek*, 188.

74 Whitney, 'Byproductive Labor', 653.

75 Hochschild, *The Managed Heart*, 17; emphasis in original.

76 Ibid., 182.

77 Arlie Russell Hochschild, *The Second Shift: Working Parents and the Revolution at Home*, Viking, 1989, 221; Encarnación Gutiérrez-Rodríguez, *Migration, Domestic Work and Affect: A Decolonial Approach on Value and the Feminization of Labor*, Routledge, 2010, 135.

78 Whitney, 'Byproductive Labor', 651.

79 Sara Farris, *In the Name of Women's Rights: The Rise of Femonationalism*, Duke University Press, 2017, 119, 130, 137.

80 Evelyn Nakano Glenn, 'From Servitude to Service Work: Historical Continuities in the Racial Division of Paid Reproductive Labor', *Signs: Journal of Women in Culture and Society* 18(1), 1992, 3.

81 Lisa Adkins, *Revisions: Gender and Sexuality in Late Modernity*, Open University Press, 2002, 84.

82 Federici, *Caliban and the Witch*, 103.

83 Wright, *Disposable Women and Other Myths*, 2, 37.

84 Robin Leidner, *Fast Food, Fast Talk: Service Work and the Routinization of Everyday Life*, University of California Press, 1993, 196.

85 Nona Glazer, *Women's Paid and Unpaid Labor: The Work Transfer in Health Care and Retailing*, Temple University Press, 1993, 12.

86 Federici, *Revolution at Point Zero*, 108.

87 Adkins, *Revisions*, 84.

88 Rebecca Selberg, *Femininity at Work: Gender, Labour, and Changing Relations of Power in a Swedish Hospital*, Arkiv förlag, 2012, 314–5.

89 Lauren Berlant, 'Cruel Optimism', *Differences: A Journal of Feminist Cultural Studies* 17(3), 2006, 21.

90 Lauren Berlant, *The Female Complaint: The Unfinished Business of Sentimentality in American Culture*, Duke University Press, 2008, 19.

91 Ruth Simpson, 'Emotional Labour and Identity Work of Men in Caring Roles', in *Gendering Emotions in Organizations*, ed.

Patricia Lewis and Ruth Simpson, Palgrave Macmillan, 2007, 65–72.

92 Steve Taylor and Melissa Tyler, 'The Exchange of Aesthetics: Women's Work and "the Gift"', *Gender, Work and Organization* 5(3), 1998, 166, 169.

93 Dalla Costa, *The Power of Women*, 30; emphasis in original.

94 Federici, *Revolution at Point Zero*, 17, 25.

95 Ibid., 15.

96 Selberg, *Femininity at Work*, 237.

4. Feminist Emotions

1 Alison Jaggar, 'Love and Knowledge: Emotion in Feminist Epistemology', in *Women and Reason*, ed. Elizabeth Harvey and Kathleen Okruhlik, University of Michigan Press, 1992, 131.

2 Arlie Russell Hochschild, *The Managed Heart: Commercialization of Human Feeling*, University of California Press, 2003, 81.

3 Jaggar, 'Love and Knowledge', 131.

4 Silvia Federici and Arlen Austin, eds., *The New York Wages for Housework Committee, 1972–1977: History, Theory and Documents*, Autonomedia, 2017, 129.

5 Jaggar, 'Love and Knowledge', 131.

6 Cited in Louise Toupin, *Wages for Housework: A History of an International Feminist Movement, 1972–77*, Pluto Press, 2018, 196.

7 Cited in ibid., 201.

8 Jaggar, 'Love and Knowledge', 132–3.

9 Ibid., 133.

10 Hochschild, *The Managed Heart*, 24, 113, 146, 167.

11 Marilyn Frye, *The Politics of Reality: Essays in Feminist Theory*, Crossing Press, 1983, 91.

12 Audre Lorde, 'The Uses of Anger', *Women's Studies Quarterly* 25(1–2), 1997, 280.

13 Federici and Austin, *New York Wages for Housework*, 125.

14 Lorde, 'The Uses of Anger', 283.

15 Hochschild, *The Managed Heart*, 129.

16 Shulamith Firestone, *The Dialectic of Sex: The Case for a Feminist Revolution*, Verso, 2015, 81.

17 Hochschild, *The Managed Heart*, 128.

18 Lorde, 'The Uses of Anger', 282.

19 Wilmette Brown, 'Black Women's Struggle against Sterilization', unpublished manuscript, box 1, Wages for Housework Special Collections, Lesbian Herstory Archive, New York, 1976, 9.

20 Kathi Weeks, 'Down with Love: Feminist Critique and the New Ideologies of Work', *Women's Studies Quarterly* 45(3–4), 2017, 55.

21 Silvia Federici, *Revolution at Point Zero: Housework, Reproduction, and Feminist Struggle*, PM Press, 2012, 18; emphasis in original.

22 Federici and Austin, *New York Wages for Housework*, 260.

23 Mariarosa Dalla Costa, *The Power of Women and the Subversion of the Community*, Falling Wall Press, 1972, 36.

24 Federici and Austin, *New York Wages for Housework*, 102.

25 Federici, *Revolution at Point Zero*, 16.

26 Ibid., 20.

27 Selma James, *Sex, Race and Class: The Perspective of Winning*, PM Press, 2012, 81; emphasis in original.

28 Karl Marx and Friedrich Engels, *The Communist Manifesto*, Vintage, 2018, 61.

29 James, *Sex, Race and Class*, 72.

30 Federici and Austin, *New York Wages for Housework*, 44.

31 Wendy Edmond and Suzie Fleming, eds., *All Work and No Pay: Women, Housework, and the Wages Due*, Falling Wall Press, 1975, 10.

32 Dalla Costa, *The Power of Women*, 26.

33 Federici and Austin, *New York Wages for Housework*, 34.

34 Federici, *Revolution at Point Zero*, 36–7.

35 James, *Sex, Race and Class*, 117.

36 Wilmette Brown, 'The Autonomy of Black Lesbian Women', unpublished manuscript, box 1, Wages for Housework Special Collections, Lesbian Herstory Archive, New York, 1976, 6–7.

37 San Francisco Wages for Housework Committee, 'An Attack on Prostitutes Is an Attack on All Women', *Lies: A Journal of Materialist Feminism* 1, 2012, 225.

38 Black Women for Wages for Housework, 'Money for Prostitutes Is Money for Black Women', *Lies: A Journal of Materialist Feminism* 1, 2012, 229; Arlen Austin and Beth Capper, ' "Wages for Housework Means Wages against Heterosexuality": On the Archives of Black Women for Wages for Housework and Wages Due Lesbians', *GLQ: A Journal of Lesbian and Gay Studies* 24(4), 2018, 452.

39 Wages Due Lesbians London, 'Supporting Statements by Wages Due Lesbians', *Lies: A Journal of Materialist Feminism* 1, 2012, 226.

40 Wages Due Lesbians Toronto, 'Lesbian and Straight', in Edmond and Fleming, *All Work and No Pay*, 21.

41 Wages Due Lesbians Toronto, 'Fucking Is Work', *The Activist: A Student Journal of Politics and Opinion* 15(1–2), 1975, 25.

42 Ruth Hall, 'Lesbianism and Power', unpublished manuscript, box 2, Wages for Housework Special Collections, Lesbian Herstory Archive, New York, 1975, 1.

43 Weeks, 'Down with Love', 49.
44 Toupin, *Wages for Housework*, 214.
45 Federici and Austin, *New York Wages for Housework*, 144.
46 Hall, 'Lesbianism and Power', 1.
47 Wages Due Lesbians Toronto, 'Fucking Is Work', 22.
48 Federici, *Revolution at Point Zero*, 24–5.
49 Hall, 'Lesbianism and Power', 2.
50 Ruth Hall, 'Lesbian Testimony Presented at the International Tribunal on Crimes Against Women', in Wages Due Lesbians Toronto, *Lesbians Organize*, Wages for Housework Campaign, 1977, 7.
51 Heather Love, *Feeling Backward: Loss and the Politics of Queer History*, Harvard University Press, 2007, 29.
52 Edmond and Fleming, *All Work and No Pay*, 23.
53 Toronto Wages for Housework Committee, *Women Speak Out*, Amazon Press, 1975, 22–3.
54 Federici, *Revolution at Point Zero*, 15.
55 Federici and Austin, *New York Wages for Housework*, 145.
56 Wages Due Lesbians Toronto, *Lesbians Organize*, 4.
57 Ibid., 12.
58 Federici, *Revolution at Point Zero*, 15.
59 Dalla Costa, *The Power of Women*, 47.
60 Ibid., 53n16.
61 Mariarosa Dalla Costa, *Women and the Subversion of the Community: A Mariarosa Dalla Costa reader*, PM Press, 2019, 54; emphasis in original.
62 Camille Barbagallo, 'The Impossibility of the Women's Strike Is Exactly Why It's So Necessary', *Women's Strike*, 14 January 2018, womenstrike.org.uk; Veronica Gago, 'The Body of Labor: A Cartography of Three Scenes from the Perspective of the Feminist Strike', *Viewpoint*, 10 June 2019, viewpointmag.com.
63 Kathi Weeks, *The Problem with Work: Feminism, Marxism, Antiwork Politics, and Postwork Imaginaries*, Duke University Press, 2011, 134.

5. A Different Feeling

1 Karl Marx, 'Critique of the Gotha Programme', in *The Political Writings*, Verso, 2019, 1030.
2 Leopoldina Fortunati, *The Arcane of Reproduction: Housework, Prostitution, Labor and Capital,* Autonomedia, 1995, 34; Mariarosa Dalla Costa, *The Power of Women and the Subversion of the Community*, Falling Wall Press, 1972, 47.

3 Margaret Prescod, 'Bringing It All Back Home', in Margaret Prescod and Norma Steele, *Black Women: Bringing It All Back Home*, Falling Wall Press, 1980, 13–14; Premilla Nadasen, *Welfare Warriors: The Welfare Rights Movement in the United States*, Routledge, 2004, 140.

4 Sara Farris, *In the Name of Women's Rights: The Rise of Femonationalism*, Duke University Press, 2017, 15.

5 Louise Toupin, *Wages for Housework: A History of an International Feminist Movement, 1972–77*, Pluto Press, 2018, 50.

6 Silvia Federici, *Revolution at Point Zero: Housework, Reproduction, and Feminist struggle*, PM Press, 2012, 38, 62.

7 Silvia Federici and Arlen Austin, eds., *The New York Wages for Housework Committee, 1972–1977: History, Theory and Documents*, Autonomedia, 2017, 21.

8 Friedrich Engels, *The Origin of the Family, Private Property and the State*, Penguin, 2010, 105.

9 Andrea Marie, 'Women and Childcare in Capitalism. Part 1: Childcare in Capitalism', *New Socialist*, 2017, newsocialist.org. uk; Toupin, *Wages for Housework*, 3.

10 Federici, *Revolution at Point Zero*, 67.

11 Ann Stewart, 'Legal Constructions of Body Work', in *Body/Sex/ Work: Intimate, Embodied and Sexualised Labour*, ed. Carol Wolkowitz, Rachel Lara Cohen, Teela Sanders, and Kate Hardy, Palgrave, 2013, 71.

12 Selma James, *Sex, Race and Class: The Perspective of Winning*, PM Press, 2012, 84.

13 Federici, *Revolution at Point Zero*, 36.

14 Arlie Russell Hochschild, *The Second Shift: Working Parents and the Revolution at Home*, Viking, 1989, 8; Christopher Carrington, *No Place like Home: Relationships and Family Life among Lesbians and Gay Men*, University of Chicago Press, 1999, 219.

15 Adrienne Rich, *Compulsory Heterosexuality and Lesbian Existence*, Onlywomen Press, 1981, 9.

16 Patricia Cain, 'Feminism and the Limits of Equality', *Georgia Law Review* 24, 1990, 805.

17 Johanna Oksala, 'Affective Labor and Feminist Politics', *Signs: Journal of Women in Culture and Society* 41(2), 2016, 300.

18 James, *Sex, Race and Class*, 197.

19 Mariarosa Dalla Costa, 'Introduction', in Giovanna Franca Dalla Costa, *The Work of Love: Unpaid Housework, Poverty and Sexual Violence at the Dawn of the 21st Century*, Autonomedia, 2008, 30.

20 Cameron Lynne Macdonald, *Shadow Mothers: Nannies, Au Pairs, and the Micropolitics of Mothering*, University of California Press, 2010, 5.

21 Dorothy Roberts, *Killing the Black Body: Race, Reproduction, and the Meaning of Liberty*, Pantheon Books, 1997; Marie, 'Women and Childcare in Capitalism'.

22 Liat Ben-Moshe, 'The Tension between Abolition and Reform', in *The End of Prisons*, ed. Mechthild Nagel and Anthony Nocella, Rodopi, 2013, 85.

23 Fred Moten and Stefano Harney, 'The University and the Undercommons: Seven Theses', *Social Text* 22(2), 2004, 114.

24 Sara Ahmed, *The Cultural Politics of Emotion*, Routledge, 2004, 128.

25 Helen Hester, *Xenofeminism*, Polity, 2018, 31, 64.

26 Wilmette Brown, 'The Autonomy of Black Lesbian Women', unpublished manuscript, box 1, Wages for Housework Special Collections, Lesbian Herstory Archive, New York, 1976; Angela Davis, *Women, Race, and Class*, Women's Press, 1981; Hazel Carby, 'White Woman Listen! Black Feminism and the Boundaries of Sisterhood', in *The Empire Strikes Back: Race and Racism in Seventies Britain*, ed. Centre for Contemporary Cultural Studies, Hutchinson, 1982; Hortense Spillers, 'Mama's Baby, Papa's Maybe: An American Grammar Book', *Diacritics* 17(2), 1987; bell hooks, *Yearning: Race, Gender, and Cultural politics*, South End Press, 1990.

27 hooks, *Yearning*, 47.

28 Carrington, *No Place like Home*; Lisa Duggan, 'The New Homonormativity: The Sexual Politics of Neoliberalism', in *Materializing Democracy: Toward a Revitalized Cultural Politics*, ed. Russ Castronovo and Dana Nelson, Duke University Press, 2002; Liz Montegary, *Familiar Perversions: The Racial, Sexual, and Economic Politics of LGBT Families*, Rutgers University Press, 2018.

29 Karl Marx and Friedrich Engels, *The Communist Manifesto*, Vintage, 2018, 54.

30 Sophie Lewis, 'Anti-fascisting', *New Inquiry*, 30 May 2019, thenewinquiry.com.

31 Jules Joanne Gleeson and Kade Doyle Griffiths, 'Kinderkommunismus', *Ritual*, 2015, available at isr.press.

32 Ibid.

33 M. E. O'Brien, 'To Abolish the Family: The Working-Class Family and Gender Liberation in Capitalist Development', *Endnotes* 5, 2020, 376.

34 Melinda Cooper, *Family Values: Between Neoliberalism and the New Social Conservatism*, Zone Books, 2017, 9–15.

35 Arlie Russell Hochschild, *The Commercialization of Intimate Life: Notes from Home and Work*, University of California Press, 2003, 171.

36 Sarah Brouillette, 'Couple Up: Review of *Family Values: Between Neoliberalism and the New Social Conservatism*', *boundary 2*, 2 June 2017.

37 Sophie Lewis, *Full Surrogacy Now: Feminism against Family*, Verso, 2019, 116.

38 Selma James, 'The American Family', in *From Feminism to Liberation*, ed. Edith Altbach, Schenkman, 1971, 196.

39 Maya Gonzalez and Jeanne Neton, 'The Logic of Gender', *Endnotes 3*, 2013, 90.

40 Karl Marx and Friedrich Engels, *The German Ideology*, Promotheus Books, 1998, 57.

41 Maya Gonzalez, 'Communization and the Abolition of Gender', in *Communization and Its Discontents: Contestation, Critique, and Contemporary Struggles*, ed. Benjamin Noys, Minor Compositions, 2012, 220, 224.

42 Shulamith Firestone, *The Dialectic of Sex: The Case for a Feminist Revolution*, Verso, 2015, 202–16.

43 James, 'The American Family', 197.

44 Ibid., 195.

45 Hester, *Xenofeminism*, 19–30.

46 Jules Joanne Gleeson, 'The Call for Gender Abolition: From Materialist Lesbianism to Gay Communism', *Blindfield Journal*, 31 July 2017, blindfieldjournal.com.

47 Gonzalez and Neton, 'The Logic of Gender', 80.

48 Selma James, 'When the Mute Speak', unpublished manuscript, box 2, Wages for Housework Special Collections, Lesbian Herstory Archive, New York, 1971.

49 Kevin Floyd, *The Reification of Desire: Toward a Queer Marxism*, University of Minnesota Press, 2009, 224.

50 Kathi Weeks, *The Problem with Work: Feminism, Marxism, Antiwork Politics, and Postwork Imaginaries*, Duke University Press, 2011, 213.

51 Firestone, *The Dialectic of Sex*, 203.

52 Kathi Weeks, *Constituting Feminist Subjects*, Cornell University Press, 1998, 145.

53 Peter Drucker, *Warped: Gay Normality and Queer Anti-capitalism*, Brill, 2015, 321; O'Brien, 'To Abolish the Family', 411.

54 José Esteban Muñoz, *Cruising Utopia: The Then and There of Queer Futurity*, New York University Press, 2009, 1.

55 Larne Abse Gogarty and Hannah Proctor, 'Communist Feelings', *New Socialist*, 13 March 2019, newsocialist.org.uk.

56 Automnia, 'Ecstasy and Warmth', *The Occupied Times* 28, 2015, 14.

57 Lewis, 'Anti-fascisting'.

58 Michèle Barrett and Mary McIntosh, *The Anti-social Family*, Verso, 2015, 149.

59 Laura Heston, 'Utopian Kinship? The Possibilities of Queer Parenting', in *A Critical Inquiry into Queer Utopias*, ed. Angela Jones, Palgrave Macmillan, 2013, 261, 263.

60 Deborah Grayson, 'Mediating Intimacy: Black Surrogate Mothers and the Law', *Critical Inquiry* 24(2), 1998; David Eng, *The Feeling of Kinship: Queer Liberalism and the Racialization of Intimacy*, Duke University Press, 2010, 94; Macdonald, *Shadow Mothers*, 13; Lewis, *Full Surrogacy Now*, 2019.

61 Federici, *Revolution at Point Zero*, 120.

62 Ibid., 115.

63 Kath Weston, *Families We Choose: Lesbians, Gays, Kinship*, Columbia University Press, 1991, 26.

64 Arlie Russell Hochschild, *The Unexpected Community: Portrait of an Old Age Subculture*, University of California Press, 1973, 21.

65 Drucker, *Warped*, 358.

66 Jane Ward, 'Radical Experiments Involving Innocent Children: Locating Parenthood in Queer Utopia', in Jones, *Critical Inquiry into Queer Utopias*, 232–3.

67 Patricia Hill Collins, 'Shifting the Center: Race, Class, and Feminist Theorizing about Motherhood', in *Representations of Motherhood*, ed. Donna Bassin, Margaret Honey, and Meryle Mahrer Kaplan, Yale University Press, 1994, 67, 70.

68 Stanlie James, 'Mothering: A Possible Black Feminist Link to Social Transformation?', in *Theorizing Black Feminisms: The Visionary Pragmatism of Black Women*, ed. Stanlie James and Abena Busia, Routledge, 1993, 47.

69 Alexis Pauline Gumbs, 'M/other Ourselves: A Black Queer Feminist Genealogy for Radical Mothering', *Revolutionary Mothering: Love on the Front Lines*, ed. Alexis Pauline Gumbs, China Martens, and Mai'a Williams, PM Press, 2016, 22.

70 Spillers, 'Mama's Baby, Papa's Maybe', 73.

71 Grace Hong, 'Existentially Surplus: Women of Color Feminism and the New Crises of Capitalism', *GLQ: A Journal of Lesbian and Gay Studies* 18(1), 2012, 92.

72 James Boggs, *The American Revolution: Pages from a Negro Worker's Notebook*, Modern Reader Paperbacks, 1963, 50.

73 O'Brien, 'To Abolish the Family', 374.

74 Nat Raha, 'Queer Capital: Marxism in Queer Theory and Post-1950 Poetics', PhD thesis, University of Sussex, 2018, 114–5.

75 Chandan Reddy, 'Home, Houses, Non-identity: *Paris Is Burning*', in *Burning Down the House: Recycling Domesticity*, ed. Rosemary George, Westview Press, 1998, 373.

76 Stephanie Coontz, *The Social Origins of Private Life: A History of American Families, 1600–1900*, Verso, 1988, 315.

77 hooks, *Yearning*, 47; Alexis Pauline Gumbs, 'We Can Learn to Mother Ourselves: The Queer Survival of Black Feminism, 1968–1996', PhD thesis, Duke University, 2010, 214.

78 Reddy, 'Home, Houses, Non-identity', 373.

79 O'Brien, 'To Abolish the Family', 416.

80 Roderick A. Ferguson, *Aberrations in Black: Toward a Queer of Color Critique*, University of Minnesota Press, 2004; Raha, 'Queer Capital', 119.

81 STAR, *Street Transvestite Action Revolutionaries: Survival, Revolt, and Queer Antagonist Struggle*, Untorelli Press, 2013.

82 Raha, 'Queer Capital', 135–7.

83 Weeks, *Constituting Feminist Subjects*, 145–50.

84 STAR, *Street Transvestite Action Revolutionaries*, 13.

85 James, *Sex, Race and Class*, 77; Toupin, *Wages for Housework*, 177, 207.

86 Lauren Berlant and Michael Warner, 'Sex in Public', *Critical Inquiry* 24(2), 1998, 558.

87 Ibid., 561.

88 James, *Sex, Race and Class*, 63, 81.

89 O'Brien, 'To Abolish the Family', 417.

90 Dolores Hayden, *The Grand Domestic Revolution: A History of Feminist Designs for American Homes*, MIT Press, 1981.

91 Alan Sears, 'Lean on Me? The Falling Rate of Friendship', *New Socialist* 59, 2006, 36–7.

92 Drucker, *Warped*, 72.

93 Weston, *Families We Choose*, 205–6.

94 Cooper, *Family Values*, 174.

95 Ibid., 211.

96 Lewis, *Full Surrogacy Now*, 22.

97 Rosemary Hennessy, *Fires on the Border: The Passionate Politics of Labor Organizing on the Mexican Frontera*, University of Minnesota Press, 2013, 206.

98 Alexandra Kollontai, *Selected Writings of Alexandra Kollontai*, Norton, 1980, 285, 289; Firestone, *The Dialectic of Sex*, 205.

99 Weeks, *Constituting Feminist Subjects*, 137–43.

100 Ruth Hall, 'Lesbianism and Power', unpublished manuscript, box 2, Wages for Housework Special Collections, Lesbian Herstory Archive, New York, 1975, 4.

101 Coontz, *Social Origins of Private Life*, 332.

102 Lewis, *Full Surrogacy Now*, 19–20.
103 Cynthia Dewi Oka, 'Mothering as Revolutionary Praxis', in Gumbs, Martens, and Williams, *Revolutionary Mothering*, 57.
104 Laurent Berlant, 'The Commons: Infrastructures for Troubling Times', *Society and Space* 34(3), 2016, 408.
105 Weeks, *Constituting Feminist Subjects*, 136.

.